Readers' Advisory Service in the Public Library

SECOND EDITION

Joyce G. Saricks
and
Nancy Brown

AMERICAN LIBRARY ASSOCIATION
Chicago and London
1997

While extensive effort has gone into ensuring the reliability
of information appearing in this book, the publisher makes
no warranty, express or implied, as to the accuracy or reliability
of the information, and does not assume and hereby disclaims
any liability to any person for any loss or damage caused by
errors or omissions in this publication.

The paper used in this publication meets the minimum
requirements of American National Standard for Information
Sciences—Permanence of Paper for Printed Library Materials,
ANSI Z39.48-1992. ∞

Library of Congress Cataloging-in-Publication Data
Saricks, Joyce G.
      Readers' advisory service in the public library /
   Joyce G. Saricks, Nancy Brown. — 2nd ed.
         p.   cm.
      Includes bibliographical references (p.   ) and indexes.
      ISBN 0-8389-0711-3 (alk. paper)
      1. Reader guidance–United States.   2. Public libraries–
   Reference services–United States.   3. Fiction in libraries.
   I. Brown, Nancy, 1940–   . II. Title.
   Z711.4.S24   1997
   025.5'2774–dc21   97-14211

Printed in the United States of America.

01   00   5   4   3   2

To Art, Kim, and Greg
for all the joy you have
and do give me

                     NB

To Chris, Brendan,
and Margaret,
who believed I could
and should do this
and were willing
to wait while I did

                     JS

CONTENTS

▓▓▓▓▓ PREFACE

I n the years since *Readers' Advisory Service in the Public Library* was first published in 1989, the library profession has experienced a dramatic increase in interest in this topic and in the way it is taught in library schools and practiced in public libraries across the country. Changes in practices, increased availability of tools, expanded knowledge of and interest in the topic, and questions from librarians convinced me that practitioners and educators would welcome a new, updated and expanded edition.

In this edition, we have added material in several areas. The important discussion of appeal, a section of chapter 4 in the first edition, now has its own chapter. The section on genre study has been greatly enlarged to reflect our growing understanding of techniques that work for us in this crucial area. A chapter on training has been added and, in order to help clarify concepts, many more specific examples of authors have been included throughout the book. The philosophy behind this revision remains consistent with that of the first edition. The aim is to introduce the user to the materials, skills, and philosophy of readers' advisory service. This book offers suggestions of techniques, rather than being prescriptive, and all material included supports a nonjudgmental, patron-oriented, skill-based readers' advisory service. As did the first edition, this revision offers topics for discussion, techniques to be modified to fit an individual library's service needs, and a philosophical basis for creating and adapting readers' advisory service.

ACKNOWLEDGMENTS

I wish to acknowledge the continuing support of the Downers Grove Public Library in promoting readers' advisory, especially Library Director Christopher Bowen, who has pushed us to continue growing and expanding our service; Assistant Director Jamie Buckovac, herself a former readers' advisor, who still enjoys working our desk; and the Library Board of Directors, who both use and support the service. The current Readers' Advisory Staff—Lora Bruggeman, Sheila Guenzer, Lynn McCullagh, Sue O'Brien, Rebecca Townsend, Terri Williams, and Carol Yarmolich—have not only challenged and inspired me; they have also read and reacted to drafts of this manuscript. For their dedication, willingness to try anything (and make it work!), faith in the goals of readers' advisory, friendship, and love of books and reading and the pleasure of sharing these, I am grateful.

Special thanks go to three tireless and dedicated readers, Sue O'Brien, Duncan Smith, and Chris Saricks. The first two offered suggestions from the perspective of professionals and experienced readers' advisors; Chris offered advice as an outsider and user of the service. Their meticulous readings and creative suggestions have been greatly valued and appreciated.

Special thanks also go to the reference staff of the Westmont Public Library, who always were able to book me into one of their study rooms where I could escape the world, and to Wolfgang Amadeus Mozart, whose music really did inspire me and keep me awake, even on days when I thought I could not write.

Thanks also to Chris, Bren, and Meg, who tolerated a year of chaos on the home front. I could not have undertaken this project without their love and support.

Finally, I want to acknowledge readers and writers around the world, librarians and others, who talk and write about the importance of fiction in their lives and in the lives of others. They keep reading alive in this electronic age and serve as an inspiration for all of us.

1 A History and Introduction

Providing readers' advisory service in public libraries is not a new idea. Organized programs have been documented since the 1920s, although their role in libraries and the philosophy on which they are based have changed dramatically over the years. In this chapter we define readers' advisory and discuss why it is important for libraries to provide this service. We also present a historical overview of past programs and the philosophy behind them, describing how current programs differ from their forerunners and fit into public libraries today.

Readers' advisory service, as discussed in this book, is a patron-oriented library service for adult fiction readers. A successful readers' advisory service is one in which knowledgeable, nonjudgmental staff help fiction readers with their reading needs. This service must be supported, encouraged, and cherished by the library administration. The public library as an institution has always championed and encouraged reading. Readers' advisors and proponents of the service subscribe wholeheartedly to the philosophy that reading, of and by itself, has intrinsic value. Books that support this belief and address the importance of reading in the lives of adults are being published in increasing numbers.[1] Readers' advisors believe that readers are best served by a library that provides both appropriate materials and a knowledgeable staff.

Libraries today offer an increasing array of services for patrons, but we remain the only agency that provides free access to books.

1

Despite increased emphasis on technology and electronic access to information, at the end of the twentieth century libraries continue to be repositories of books and information in a variety of forms. During this time of technological advances, librarians are discovering that while technology provides tools that facilitate our access to information and help us better serve our patrons, many of our users rely on the library for more than information alone. Students come to gather statistics for reports, but they also seek books that reflect or help them temporarily escape the issues they face daily. Adults, both men and women, come to libraries for more than stock quotations, health information, and how-to information; they also request fiction that challenges, inspires, or takes them away when the world becomes too much.[2] Studies show that more than sixty percent of users come to the library for leisure reading.[3] Fiction constitutes the largest portion of material sought by that group, and readers' advisory staff assists these readers.

Although a growing number of public libraries acknowledge the importance of assisting fiction readers with their leisure reading queries, statistical evidence of the importance of fiction and fiction readers in public libraries is limited. Traditional public library statistical data, such as high circulation figures or a significant percentage of users, cannot be cited as there have been, to our knowledge, no national research projects based on circulation data or wide-ranging user studies that give percentages for public library fiction use. Individual libraries have statistics that support the popularity of fiction in their institutions, but no large-scale compilation exists at this time. Despite this surprising lack of statistical data, the generally accepted assumption in the professional literature and by librarians in the field is that fiction circulation is substantial. This conclusion is borne out by data from North Carolina, which indicates that adult fiction accounts for thiry-seven percent of all book circulation.[4]

Despite the lack of extensive circulation data, there are powerful pragmatic reasons for a library to provide readers' advisory service for its patrons, as well as a considerable amount of anecdotal evidence of the popularity of fiction. Concerning the latter, most practicing librarians will attest to the increasing number of patrons interested in reading fiction. One indicator of this popularity, which has been discussed extensively in the current library literature, is the pressure placed on public libraries to provide "enough" fiction best-sellers. In fact, to meet the demand for fiction in general, libraries spend a sizable portion of their budgets on selecting, purchasing, processing, housing, shelving, and generally maintaining their fiction collections. Given this high patron demand and significant budgeting commitment, libraries need to address the concerns of their fiction readers more directly. If the public library as a whole is perceived not merely as a self-service institution in which users are expected to make choices with only minimal assistance, it follows that libraries need to provide trained, knowledgeable staff to work with fiction readers, as well as with those seeking help with the nonfiction collection.

Another compelling argument in favor of providing readers' advisory service arises from the organization of the fiction collection, which by its very nature creates some special problems that require trained assistance. For instance, patrons who walk into the library in the mood for a light, quick, escapist book may be confronted by thousands of books organized alphabetically by author. This arrangement is a little daunting, not to mention frustrating. The alphabetical arrangement of the fiction collection is a major barrier for many readers; often, finding the specific kind of book they want is nearly impossible. Even when readers have the title of a book they have enjoyed, how can they find a similar book? The readers' advisor provides this vital link between the library's fiction material and readers.

History of Readers' Advisory Services

Providing readers' advisory service is not a new idea. By reviewing it origins, we can identify the underlying principles and practices that form the basis of present-day readers' advisory service. Readers' advisory service experienced its first flourishing in United States public libraries in the 1920s through the 1940s. Robert Ellis Lee, in his study, *Continuing Education for Adults through the American Public Library, 1833–1964*, describes three phases in the development of reader guidance, or readers' advisory, between 1922 and 1940.[5] The first phase, from 1922 to 1926, saw structured readers' advisory service begun in seven urban public libraries: Chicago, Cincinnati, Cleveland, Detroit, Indianapolis, Milwaukee, and Portland, Oregon. Reader guidance, covering both fiction and nonfiction, was a special and specialized service that was provided separately from other library services. Advisors met with patrons in private interviews, often in offices set aside for that purpose, to determine an appropriate reading plan. The advisors then prepared "individualized reading courses for persons who wished to read systematically to meet the practical needs of daily living."[6]

During the second phase, from 1927 to 1935, both the effectiveness and the scope of the service were increased. It was during this period also that the Adult Education Roundtable was formed and first met at the 1927 ALA Annual Conference. ALA's Reading with a Purpose courses, which consisted of books and "annotated lists of books on special topics," were featured in public libraries.[7]

By 1935, forty-four libraries provided a readers' advisory service. Jennie M. Flexner of the New York Public Library, which initiated its readers' advisory service in 1929, published numerous articles and two books about that library's program. These studies provide useful insights into the kind of work being done at that time. Readers were interviewed extensively by librarians about their reading interests, both to aid in developing individualized lists and to ascertain patrons' reading levels. While this approach sounds very similar to that used in present-day readers' advisory interviews, the judgmental suppositions made about patrons then are in direct contrast to today's attitude. For example, the patron who named *Atlantic Monthly* as a magazine read regularly was felt to have better reading skills than one who read the *Saturday Evening Post* or *Time*.[8] After the interview, an annotated reading list was prepared and then mailed to the reader, who would seek out the books in the local branch library.

The growth of the idea of readers' advisory in public libraries during this second phase was attributed to three causes: "(1) the increased number of professional workers in public libraries; (2) the increased idleness and leisure caused by the Depression . . . ; and (3) the beginning of systematic research relating to problems of adult reading."[9] The studies of adult reading and readability that were carried out during this time provided a basis for the techniques librarians used in linking book selection with "the reading interests, habits, and abilities of adults" and thus made readers' advisory services more effective.[10]

The third phase, from 1936 to 1940, saw the broadening of readers' advisory within libraries. Subject specialists worked with readers' advisors in formulating reading lists. While this development indicated an expansion of the readers' advisory service, it also pointed out the extensive reading background required by librarians in preparing individualized, annotated book lists. As the demand for the service increased, providing these lists became more difficult.

During this time, more than thirty articles describing aspects of readers' advisory service appeared in professional journals, in addition to several full-length books. One study, *Helping the Reader toward Self-education,* identified seventy reader types and classed them by occupation, race, sex, and personality traits.[11] Ranging from The Timid and Inferior-Feeling Person, The Low-Brow, and Tenement Dwellers to The Ambitious Person and the Sophisticated Woman, each type was listed with three to four book titles considered appropriate reading suggestions. For instance, The Unskilled Worker was advised to read Steinbeck's *Of Mice and Men;* for The Coward, Conrad's *Lord Jim* was suggested; and The Criminal in the Making was advised to read Dreiser's *An American Tragedy.* We can only marvel at the presumption involved in making such judgments about the reader's character and then persuading each type to read and benefit from the chosen titles. This moralistic, didactic tone contrasts strikingly with that of the present. It seems amazing to readers' advisors today that librarians of the past could make the smug assumption that their reading suggestions would result in dramatic self-improvement in the readers. For those wishing to read further about this and other studies on the history of readers' advisory service, see the Bibliography of historical sources at the end of this book.

World War II and the accompanying reduction in leisure time dramatically decreased requests for readers' advisory service and some libraries discontinued it.[12] By 1949 readers' advisory was clearly "going out of fashion."[13] However, a Reading Guidance Institute held at the University of Wisconsin Library School in 1965 indicated continued, although perhaps peripheral, interest in the subject.[14]

The underlying concern of librarians involved in these earlier readers' advisory services was the role of the public library in adult continuing education. Librarians saw readers' advisory service as a means of helping adults meet their need for further learning. In the words of Lee Regan, "What was stressed in these early efforts was (1) the unique opportunity which libraries offered for continuous, informal adult education; and (2) the friendly and close relationship which reader's advisers formed with patrons."[15]

"Friendly and close" though the relationship between librarian and patron might have been, the approach was clearly didactic. The aim of the readers' advisory service was to move readers toward classic works, to outline a plan of reading that would be educational, not recreational. Saddled with this worthy but formidable goal of providing materials for adult continuing education and expected to fulfill almost a tutorial role with patrons, readers' advisors who subscribed to this philosophy found that the work involved in providing this service eventually became too burdensome. Librarians were unable to meet the demands for so many individually prepared and extensive reading lists. Out of necessity, the lists became more standardized, and some of the individual contact was lost.[16]

Despite differences between readers' advisory of the past and present, both in purpose and in attitude, some threads can be traced linking the early services to current practice. First, readers' advisors then and now have acknowledged the difficulty in discovering what it is that patrons are seeking when they ask for reading suggestions. An expertise in interviewing in order to discover patron interests and to match them with appropriate authors and titles continues to be vital to the process. Second, readers' advisors, past and present, need a general knowledge of fiction, an ability to recognize the quality of the books they suggest, and the ability to describe books well, both orally and in writing. Finally, present-day readers' advisors concur with their historical predecessors about the importance of the personal relationship between librarian and reader, even if these librarians would disagree about the nature of that relationship. In their 1934 study of the readers' advisory service at the New York Public Library, Flexner and Edge discuss, in terms with which we all can agree, What is a readers' adviser?[17] Such a librarian has, among other things, "a wide acquaintance with the insides of books . . . ," the ability to discuss individual books with readers, and the ability "to share his enthusiasm over certain books."[18] In short, a readers' advisor, past and present, is "a librarian at the disposal of the reader, trying to make easier and more satisfying the connection between the reader and books."[19]

Readers' Advisory Today

Librarians today find themselves in the midst of a readers' advisory renaissance. Interest in and enthusiasm for providing readers' advisory in public libraries have grown enormously in the last decade. Readers' advisors, and other librarians interested in programs related to the fiction collection, once sought in vain for relevant programs at national conferences; now we find them in increasing numbers, especially at conferences sponsored by the

Public Library Association (PLA). In 1996, PLA in Portland offered nine programs specifically related to readers' advisory—all to overflow crowds—as well as three popular talk tables related to this field. In addition, popular fiction writers Jayne Ann Krentz and Jean Auel drew over one thousand librarians to the two luncheon programs. The American Library Association's Reference Users Services Association (RUSA) established a readers' advisory committee in 1994. Within its first three years, the committee has presented a program on readers' advisory training (ALA June, 1996), published a bibliography of readers' advisory resources, and planned a program on readers' advisors and the Internet for ALA in summer of 1997.[20]

Many state conferences, too, have offered programs for librarians interested in readers' advisory. A compilation of conference papers dealing with readers' advisory and originally presented at the Illinois Library Association conference in 1995 will be published in 1997.[21] In addition, library systems and individual libraries have focused on readers' advisory with extensive training programs provided by in-house staff as well as outside experts. All of this speaks to a growing professional recognition of the importance of readers' advisory in our public libraries and of the necessity of training for staff who provide this service.

Research in this field continues to grow as well. Both scholarly and practical articles appear in increasing numbers in library literature. In addition, in the last few years Neal-Schuman has published two scholarly compilations of research on readers' advisory.[22] Even the Library of Congress, in conjunction with Online Computer Library Center (OCLC), is working to improve subject access to works of fiction by expanding the range of subject headings assigned to adult fiction titles.

Organizations of readers' advisory librarians have also flourished. An example of this type of group is the Adult Reading Round Table in Illinois, with over two hundred members. It recently celebrated ten years of providing quality programs to Chicago-area readers' advisors. This group presents three readers' advisory programs yearly—a genre/literature program, nuts and bolts (how to . . .), and a small group discussion for which each participant brings and discusses a book on a specific topic. This group also produces a newsletter three times yearly and an annotated book list each year. In addition, members may participate in a two-year genre study, led by a member of the organization. We advocate that librarians seek out others interested in readers' advisory service and form such groups, not only for the continuing education aspects of the meetings, but also for the opportunities this activity provides to interact with others. From the meetings and the contacts we have made, we have developed a strong support group of librarians with whom we can discuss both readers' advisory philosophy and patron questions, as well as foster further commitment to providing quality readers' advisory service.

Readers' advisory practices in the 1990s have also changed significantly from their pedagogical origins. The relationship between readers and librarians is now much less didactic. By and large, public library patrons are interested primarily in talking to librarians about recreational reading, chiefly fiction. Rather than "elevating the masses," readers' advisors strive to be knowledgeable about fiction—particularly that which is popular in their libraries—and to respond with perception and insight to the reading interests of their patrons.

Qualifications for readers' advisors and staffing requirements for a department are also seen in a different light today. Although in the past entire departments were devoted solely to readers' advisory, only a few libraries have that luxury today. Readers' advisory can be done on some level wherever there are people who care about reading and who want to help others find reading materials of interest to them. A readers' advisory service can be part of a reference or a circulation department's activities. Readers' advisors need not have professional library degrees; our own experience, as well as new research, confirms that trained paraprofessionals can be excellent readers' advisors.[23]

Providing Readers' Advisory

The two keys to providing readers' advisory in any library setting, regardless of library size or staffing, are commitment to serving fiction readers and a responsive attitude toward readers, no matter what they enjoy reading. While anyone who cares about books and reading can suggest books, a library that claims to offer a readers' advisory service has an obligation to provide knowledgeable staff, as well as to make an ongoing commitment of time and library resources.

In addition to the desire to make a "connection between the reader and books," attributes of readers' advisors include a willingness to read widely, a knowledge of the interests of the library's patrons, and a familiarity with popular genres. Readers' advisors of today commit time and effort to providing this service, a great deal of it spent in reading and study. Time also must be set aside to master the techniques of the readers' advisory interview, to learn to talk about books with readers, to gain familiarity with the range of popular fiction, and to create tools to help readers' advisors assist readers. These subjects will be covered in the following chapters.

Before we discuss specific readers' advisory techniques, some important terms, which we use in a nontraditional way, need to be clarified in order to prevent confusion about our meaning and intention. First, the term *appeal* refers to those elements in a book, whether definable or just understood, that make readers enjoy the book. We use the designation *similar authors* to mean a group of authors whose works share elements that appeal to the same readers. When discussing fiction, we use the term *genre* to mean any sizable group of fiction authors and/or specific titles that have similar characteristics and appeal; these are books written to a particular, specific pattern. In discussing fiction, we often use the term *good books* as a form of shorthand to mean novels that are enjoyable to read and in which the writing meets a recognized quality standard. Admittedly, this may be an unstated and rather nebulous standard, but it is one most professionals use, if perhaps intuitively, to judge quality fiction.

In comparing the philosophy of readers' advisory past and present, we can see that it is primarily the attitude toward the reader that has changed. Readers' advisors in the 1920s and 1930s saw themselves as educators; they knew what was good for readers and led them in specific directions. Readers' advisors today see themselves as links between fiction readers and books, just as reference librarians are the connection between users and nonfiction materials. Libraries already allot resources—both time and money—to developing and maintaining their fiction collections; such expenditures justify a similar commitment of staff to make the collection as accessible as possible to readers. In the next chapter, we examine reference books and other tools that aid readers' advisors in providing this service.

Notes

1. For example, Lynne Sharon Schwartz, *Ruined by Reading: A Life in Books* (Boston: Beacon, 1996); Sven Birkerts, *The Gutenberg Elegies: The Fate of Reading in an Electronic Age* (Boston: Faber, 1994); Daniel Pennac, *Better than Life* (Toronto: Coach House, 1994); and Robert Coles, *The Call of Stories: Teaching and the Moral Imagination* (Boston: Houghton, 1989).

2. In *Adventure, Mystery, and Romance: Formula Stories as Art and Popular Culture* (Chicago: Univ. of Chicago Pr., 1976), author John G. Cawelti discusses in depth the importance and role of formulaic literature in our lives.

3. John N. Berry III, "Most People Come for the Fun of It," *Library Journal* 118 (October 1993): 6.

4. Kenneth Shearer, "Reflections on the Findings and Implications for Practice," in *Guiding the Reader to the Next Book,* ed. Kenneth Shearer (New York: Neal-Schuman, 1996), 171.

5. Robert Ellis Lee, *Continuing Education for Adults through the American Public Library, 1833–1964* (Chicago: American Library Assn., 1966), 57–60.

6. Ibid., p. 57.

7. Lee Regan, "Status of Reader's Advisory Service," *RQ* 12 (spring 1973): 227.

8. Jennie M. Flexner and Byron C. Hopkins, *Readers' Advisers at Work: A Survey of Development in the New York Public Library* (New York: American Assn. for Adult Education, 1941), 21.

9. Lee, *Continuing Education,* 58.

10. Ibid., 59.

11. John Chancellor, Miriam D. Tompkins, and Hazel I. Medway, *Helping the Reader toward Self-education* (Chicago: American Library Assn., 1938).

12. Lee, *Continuing Education,* 60.

13. Regan, *Status,* 230.

14. Ibid.

15. Ibid., 227.

16. Ibid., 229.

17. Jennie M. Flexner and Sigrid A. Edge, *A Readers' Advisory Service* (New York: American Assn. for Adult Education, 1934), 50–57.

18. Ibid., 53.

19. Ibid., 51.

20. Readers' Advisory Committee, "Readers' Advisory Reference Tools: A Suggested List of Fiction Sources for All Libraries," *RQ* 36 (winter 1996): 206–29.

21. Ted Balcom, ed., *Serving Readers* (Fort Atkinson, Wis.: Highsmith, 1997).

22. Kathleen de la Pena McCook and Gary O. Rolstad, eds., *Developing Readers' Advisory Services: Concepts and Commitments* (New York: Neal-Schuman, 1993); and Kenneth D. Shearer, ed., *Guiding the Reader to the Next Book* (New York: Neal-Schuman, 1996).

23. Research in North Carolina confirms that there is no evidence that professionals provide better readers' advisory service than do paraprofessionals. See Kenneth D. Shearer and Pauletta B. Bracy, "Readers' Advisory Services: A Response to the Call for More Research," *RQ* 33 (summer 1994): 457.

2 Reference Sources

E very readers' advisory department depends on its collection of reference sources. In this chapter, we begin by looking at two standard reference sources, with an eye to the way in which they can be used most profitably by readers' advisors. In the second section, which highlights additional reference sources, we discuss the features of these resources that make them particularly useful for readers' advisory work; we then give some examples of reference resources that we feel exhibit these features. In the third section, we describe a Popular Fiction List—a checklist of authors and genres popular in our library—that we have developed and use as a reference source. In discussing how and why we created this list, as well as in sharing our experiences in using it, we explain how any library can devise its own list to reflect its collection and patron reading interests. In the final section, we discuss the cooperative nature of readers' advisory and the importance of staff and colleagues as an often over-looked but valuable resource.

Two Sources Readers' Advisors Cannot Live Without

Fiction Catalog

If you can have only one reference book nearby while doing readers' advisory, choose *Fiction Catalog,* which is an indispensable aid as a selection guide, reference tool, and source of suggestions for readers.[1] *Fiction Catalog* is issued hardbound with four annual paper supplements. Currently, the hardbound editions appear every five years. The thirteenth edition lists almost six thousand titles of classic and contemporary works of adult fiction, including novelettes and composite works. The new editions are not cumulative, although many titles reappear in subsequent editions. The reason for this is that titles to be included in each edition are selected by a panel of librarians from public library systems. These librarians receive a list of possible titles, seek a consensus from librarians in their systems, and vote for the ones they believe should be included. They need not have read the books, nor do they need to consider whether titles have been listed in previous editions or supplements.

Fiction Catalog is divided into two sections: a main entry section and an index of titles and subjects. The main section is arranged alphabetically by author, then title. Information about editions, ISBN numbers for in-print books, number of pages, and sequels (where appropriate) are all part of the bibliographic data. Each entry includes a descriptive summary and an excerpt from critical remarks, usually from a review. Readers usually find that the summary gives enough information to let them decide whether they have read or want to read a particular book. *Fiction Catalog* is definitely a book we can put in patrons' hands; with a brief introduction, they can use this reference tool very satisfactorily on their own. For the readers' advisor, simply reading these plot summaries is useful, as they provide an example to follow in formulating one's own annotations. The plot is summarized concisely, in terms that help readers' advisors elucidate the book's appeal to readers.

While the alphabetical entry section makes up the bulk of *Fiction Catalog,* the real fun comes in using and perusing the Title and Subject Index. This index is a gold mine, for it provides subject and genre access to the individual book descriptions in the main section. The number and variety of subjects included are amazing. Among the many subjects listed are geographic places, historical periods and events, people, life-styles (e.g., SOCIETY NOVELS, POVERTY, FARM LIFE), genres, and literary types (e.g., DIALECT STORIES, STREAM OF CONSCIOUSNESS, PARODIES). There are numerous *see* and *see also* references to direct the user. The information gained by reading through the subject headings list alone—a practice that probably should be required yearly of all readers' advisors—will impress anyone who has tried to find books within a particular subject or genre.

Fiction Catalog may be used profitably in several ways. At this point in time, it is the best single source we know for historical fiction, as it provides summaries of all titles, sequel information, and extensive subject access. The annual supplements keep readers' advisors up-to-date on additional titles. The subject index lists not only historical events, such as WORLD WAR, 1939–1945, but it also subdivides events into categories. For instance, under WORLD WAR, 1939–1945, are subheadings for geographic places, as well as specific topics such as AERIAL OPERATIONS, NAVAL OPERATIONS—SUBMARINE, and ATROCITIES. Historical periods are listed under the names of countries. Specialized topics can be accessed with a little ingenuity; for example, by comparing the author and title list under ENGLAND 16TH CENTURY and that under COURTS AND COURTIERS—ENGLAND, we will have a list of authors and titles that use sixteenth-century English court backgrounds.

To find lists of genre authors and titles, we need some familiarity with which subjects in *Fiction Catalog* relate to certain genres. To find Espionage Thrillers, for example, try the headings INTERNATIONAL INTRIGUE, SPIES, and SECRET SERVICE. Under MYSTERY AND DETECTIVE STORIES, authors and titles are listed by the location in which the Mystery novel is set. To find an author when all we have is the name of the fictional detective, look under the subject DETECTIVES, where fictional detectives and their creators are listed. This list is a great boon when a reader wants Mysteries involving a certain detective but cannot remember the author's name.

Some very hard-to-find categories of genre and style are also included. For instance, CHEERFUL STORIES is a good source for readers who prefer the Gentle Reads (books without sex, violence, or strong language). NOVELETTES is for readers of short books. Other out-of-the-ordinary subject classifications include: ALLEGORIES, AUTOBIOGRAPHICAL STORIES, both DIARIES (STORIES ABOUT) and DIARIES (STORIES IN DIARY FORM), PHILOSOPHICAL NOVELS, PICARESQUE NOVELS, SOCIETY NOVELS, UNFINISHED NOVELS, and STORIES WITHIN A NOVEL. These headings are difficult, if not impossible, to find anywhere else.

The subject index is not only a source of authors who write about particular subjects but also an easy way to discover book titles and authors when the reader can describe only the story or setting. If we feel that the book might be included in *Fiction Catalog*, we try all the subject access words that occur to us. The best advice is not to give up if a reader is trying to identify a book but does not remember the author or title. There are so many subject access points that one is sure to work.

Readers' advisors can use *Fiction Catalog*'s subject index in several other valuable ways. If we are trying to find similar authors, spending some time with this index can help us make connections. If, for example, John Grisham and William J. Coughlin each have several titles listed under the heading LAW AND LAWYERS, we can investigate further both in the main entries and in the books themselves to determine if these authors have the same appeal. The subject index is also a source of inspiration for topics and titles for book lists. If we find ourselves with more requests for a type of book, such as Southern Fiction, than we can fill, *Fiction Catalog* provides a ready-made list for collection development. We can increase the usefulness of *Fiction Catalog* if we indicate in the margin of the author section those titles our libraries own. It is also helpful to note in the Title and Subject Index, under frequently requested headings, the books that the library owns. When we mark our holdings, patrons can easily see what we have and what they therefore might expect to find on the shelf.

There are times when we have been glad to have more than one edition of *Fiction Catalog* on hand. Not only might we have more than one reader wanting to use *Fiction Catalog* at a time; but when we are creating book lists and bookmarks, we will want to make extensive use of all the editions. The hardcover edition neither cumulates all titles from the annual supplements nor necessarily includes titles from previous editions. Since each edition is started from scratch with a new voting list, some titles will be eliminated; therefore, to put together a complete list in any subject area, we need to look in older editions, too. Some subject headings, such as CHARACTER STUDIES and FIRST PERSON, have been discontinued but may be just what we need. Because H. W. Wilson Company does not sell the previous editions, it pays to save all old copies.

While a wonderful resource, *Fiction Catalog* has some deficiencies. The catalog's usefulness would be increased to readers' advisors tenfold if the subject lists for each title were added to the main entry. If we know what subject headings have been assigned to a particular author, it helps us categorize the author's work and provide access to similar authors under those same subject headings. In addition, a list of subject headings that have been dropped or added to each edition would be useful. Finally, electronic access to the data in *Fiction Catalog* would make it an even more valuable resource for readers' advisory. While H. W. Wilson has made most of its reference data available on-line for years, it has ignored *Fiction Catalog*. The ability to search electronically, to link headings, and to see all headings listed for individual titles would dramatically increase the resource's usefulness to readers' advisors. Failure to provide electronic access may lessen *Fiction Catalog*'s importance as a resource in coming years, as other products that do provide such access take its place in the library market.

Genreflecting

Betty Rosenberg taught a library school course called Reading Interests that was designed to help future librarians understand "common readers" and their tastes. Her book, *Genreflecting*, grew out of the syllabus for that course. Diana Tixier Herald joined Rosenberg as coauthor of the third edition in 1991. Since Rosenberg's death in 1993, Herald has taken on sole responsibility for *Genreflecting*, and the fourth edition was published in 1995.[2]

Genreflecting is organized by genre and each section includes a definition of the genre, followed by explanations of subgenres and lists of authors for each subgenre, often with representative titles. Indexes to authors, titles, subjects, series, and characters provide access to the wealth of information contained in each chapter. Although this reference work can and should be supplemented by as wide a range of books on individual genres as possible, it stands alone as *the* starting point in learning about and working with genre fiction.

After an opening chapter on the nature of genre fiction and its relationship to readers, libraries, and publishing, a chapter is devoted to each of seven genres: Western, Crime, Adventure, Romance, Science Fiction, Fantasy, and Horror. Each chapter includes two sections: Themes and Types, and Topics.

The first section, Themes and Types, offers the most concise and elucidating discussion of individual genres that we have found in any source. Herald's descriptions alone make this a reference guide not to be missed. She delineates the pattern inherent in each genre—that which distinguishes it from other genres—and then identifies and discusses each genre's particular appeal to readers. Having all this information on the most popular genres in one place makes *Genreflecting* an excellent resource, but the fact that she also includes representative authors and titles for each of more than 180 subgenres makes this book invaluable for students, readers, and readers' advisors. For example, in the chapter on Westerns, she lists and describes authors and titles for more than forty subgenres—both traditional and nontraditional—ranging from Town

Marshal and The Indian to Adult Western and The Indian Today, and not forgetting The Singular Woman and Romance, as well as Comedy and Parody.

The second section of each genre chapter, Topics, includes a wide variety of interesting and useful information. Here Herald includes lists of classic authors, "bests" within the genre, anthologies, bibliographies, histories, criticism, encyclopedias, films, book clubs, manuals, and more, including a list of titles that are among her personal favorites.

Beyond its lucid and comprehensive genre definitions and examples of genre fiction, what makes *Genreflecting* invaluable is the attitude Betty Rosenberg established in the first edition in 1982. The first edition's epigraph, *Rosenberg's First Law of Reading: Never apologize for your reading tastes*, sets the tone for the book and has appeared in each subsequent edition. Rosenberg and Herald are readers, and their remarks come from the viewpoint of readers who enjoy genre fiction, not necessarily from that of librarians or readers' advisors. Rosenberg wrote in the Introduction to the first edition, "Genre fiction is not to be taken seriously and analyzed to death. It should be written about by those who enjoy it."[3] Rosenberg's approach to each genre, carried on by Herald, is nonjudgmental; she simply addresses the pattern within the genre and discusses its appeal to readers. She also counteracts some people's disdain for the tastes of the "common reader," for their perception of genre fiction as the bottom rung of the fiction ladder. She unabashedly advocates reading for pleasure and attempts in this book to give librarians an understanding of genre fiction so that they can provide assistance to other readers who enjoy this genre. Under Rosenberg's tutelage, reading and enjoying genre fiction become virtues, not closet vices. Herald has maintained this tone in subsequent editions.

It was partly Rosenberg's attitude that initially made *Genreflecting* such a useful tool for us. The book came as a godsend when we were just starting our readers' advisory department. Betty Rosenberg put us on the right track by giving us a basic understanding of different genres so that we could talk with interested readers with a real appreciation for their interest and a commitment to serving them. We spent a lot of time reading and rereading chapters and author/title lists, acquainting ourselves with themes and examples. Rosenberg's inviting comments greatly expanded our lists of wonderful books we simply had to read.

We are still using *Genreflecting* much as we did during those first years. It is the place we go to refresh our memories about a genre and all of its subgenres or to acquaint ourselves with an unfamiliar genre. It is an almost endless source of reading suggestions for us and for patrons. We use this reference tool frequently to find authors similar to patrons' favorites as well as lists of authors who write a certain kind of book. Since Herald usually lists titles along with authors, she provides a means for starting a reader on an author with whom we are unfamiliar. If we look up all of the page references under an author in the Author/Title Index, we can find examples of the various types of genres in which an author writes. The theme and subgenre lists are also good starting places for generating ideas for bookmarks and annotated book lists. This book is particularly valuable for collection development in a genre area. We use the "best" lists or refer to lists of special themes that relate to the collections on which we are working. The bibliographies of other genre reference books in each chapter provide yet another good starting place for the study of genres and the expansion of a reference collection. The fourth edition of *Genreflecting* is also accessible electronically on Carl Corporation's *NoveList,* an electronic readers' advisory tool described later in this chapter. In addition, Herald maintains a Web page on which she updates *Genreflecting,* provides links to other sites of interest to readers' advisors and genre fiction readers, and reviews titles she believes her readers might be interested in.

Since we mentioned the usefulness of *Fiction Catalog's* subject index, it is interesting to note how *Genreflecting's* Subject Index differs from it. Both provide subject access to fiction, but *Genreflecting's* index is limited to genre fiction and is the first place we look when we are doing a subject search for a genre reader or working on a genre book list in one of the genres included. We can find Mysteries and names of individual detectives in *Fiction Catalog,* but *Genreflecting* breaks the genre down into many additional and more specific subcategories. In Romance, for example, *Fiction Catalog* lists a wide range of authors and titles—both classic and popular—under the headings LOVE STORIES, LOVE AFFAIRS, COURTSHIP, LOVERS, and GOTHIC ROMANCES. *Genreflecting,* on the other hand, provides direct access to the entire scope of the Romance genre by listing subgenres under the heading in the index, and to more authors and titles within that specific genre than does *Fiction Catalog.* Certainly, readers of Regency Romances are better served by *Genreflecting,* which has a separate indexed list of these authors, than by *Fiction Catalog,* where Regencies are included but not specifically identified in the extensive list under ENGLAND—19TH CENTURY. As we become more familiar with both reference sources, we develop a feel for which source does what. *Genreflecting* provides greater access to those topics within a genre that are often just what the fans want to read—a Medical Horror novel or Legal Thriller, for example.

For both novice and experienced readers' advisors, *Genreflecting* is a "must" read. It is a remarkable reference book that provides a framework for learning more about genres, an extensive list of authors and titles to suggest to interested readers, and an example of the attitude that inspires and sustains readers' advisors. Although *Genreflecting* is certainly useful and comprehensive, Herald herself admonishes, "It should be used as an introduction in need of continual supplementation."4 *Genreflecting* provides a broad and firm foundation for the readers' advisor, but it is only a starting place. As we readers' advisors read more within and about genres, we sometimes find that we want to refine *Genreflecting*'s classification of authors within genres, and we will discover others to add. We stretch our own understanding of and our ability to discriminate among themes and subgenres as we compare our own lists to those in *Genreflecting*. While *Genreflecting* is the perfect starting place for developing a thorough understanding of genre fiction, readers' advisors must watch for and note changes in the genres and add new authors and subgenres as they appear. Herald understands this and assists us by providing updates on her Web page.

Additional Reference Sources

Fiction Catalog and *Genreflecting* are the basic tools for readers' advisory work. All readers' advisors need to be experienced and well versed in using them. They will be the first place to go in answering many readers' queries and most useful in training new readers' advisors. However, we all need additional reference materials that deal with fiction authors and their work. How many resources and which ones we purchase will depend on our own library's budget, collection, and—most important—the needs and interests of our readers. In this section, we first outline the features to look for in a readers' advisory reference tool, summarized in Figure 2.1. Then we describe specific resources that fit these criteria. At the danger of repeating ourselves, we cannot state too emphatically that our reference sources must fit both our needs and the interests of our reading public. To a great extent, our readers define the type of reference sources we need.

Figure 2.1
What to Look for in Commercially Produced Readers'
Advisory Reference Sources

1. Access points/indexes.
2. Plot summaries.
3. Evaluative material about books:

   Characteristics of the author's works.

   Best and/or most representative titles.

   Where to start new readers.
4. Point of view from which written.

When we examine a potential readers' advisory reference book, we look first at the type of access provided to its contents. Any index is better than no index, but we firmly believe that author and title access in resource books should be made mandatory by an act of Congress. Note any books that give access beyond author and title—especially useful are access by pseudonym, character name, and subject. For example, check Mystery resources for access by detective or main character, by country, by subject (e.g., lawyers, doctors, antiques, universities), and by type (e.g., police procedural, amateur sleuth). The book version of Gale's *What Do I Read Next?* (discussed below) has a wealth of useful indexes.

Certain other features can make a resource particularly useful. Treasure any book that gives plot summaries. These can help readers decide either whether they have already read a particular book or whether they might be interested in reading it. *Fiction Catalog,* as mentioned above, is a good example of this type of source.

It is worth taking notice if a book discusses authors' styles or the characteristics of authors' works. Just reading through descriptions that characterize particular authors will familiarize us with those authors—even ones we have not read—and help us in describing those authors specifically and authors in general. In addition, if comparisons are made between authors, and similarities and differences are pointed out, we have a real find. This type of information can be enormously helpful when we and the patron are on the trail of possible similar authors. The titles in the *St. James Guides* series, discussed in more detail below, often help readers make these connections.

A reference book that provides a judgment on an author's best or most representative work gives us a title to suggest when we are starting a reader on a new author. We also watch for books, such as *Genreflecting,* that include core collections or reading lists, as they provide a place to begin the study of a genre and serve also as a resource guide for collection development.

Often, it is the attitude of the author that makes one reference resource more helpful than another to readers' advisors. Janet and Jonathan Husband's *Sequels* and Herald's *Genreflecting* are perfect examples of reference sources written by people who love books and reading and thus write from the reader's point of view.[5] From this type of source, the readers' advisor gains an appreciation for a title or genre as well as the enthusiasm of readers of that title or genre.

How do we find reference sources like these? With the features we have discussed in mind, we advise scouring your own shelves. We were surprised to see that we already owned several very useful sources, but we were unaware of their scope until we started looking for background material on genres and authors. We found that it is best to keep these sources close to the public service desk; that way we can introduce readers to them as well as use them for reference. Genre readers love books about their particular reading passion; we find them poring over these books and making lists of authors and titles they want to try. For a more comprehensive list of readers' advisory resources, consult the extensive bibliography, covering more than eighty readers' advisory resources in book form, compiled by the American Library Association's Readers' Advisory Committee, which is part of the Reference Users Services Association (RUSA).[6] The list is divided into three sections—Core, Expanded, and Comprehensive Collections—and includes information on ways in which each source is useful to readers' advisors. Although this is an excellent basic list, there are likely new editions of the included titles and certainly new titles worth considering.

The following resources exhibit some of the features we recommend. For instance, the *St. James Guide* series (formerly the *Twentieth-Century* series) is a good example of what to look for in a readers' advisory reference source. The series includes:

> *Twentieth-Century Romance and Historical Writers*
>
> *St. James Guide to Crime and Mystery Writers*
>
> *St. James Guide to Fantasy Writers*
>
> *St. James Guide to Science Fiction Writers*
>
> *Twentieth-Century Western Writers*[7]

Although technically it is not, we consider *Contemporary Novelists* to be part of this series because it has a similar layout and features, and it can be used in the same way as the others by readers' advisors.[8]

The resources in the *St. James Guide* series include only selected authors. The main entries, arranged alphabetically by author, contain thoughtful, signed critical essays that describe book themes, authors' styles, and individual titles (usually the best or most representative), and often give selected plot summaries. Similar authors are occasionally mentioned. Directed at potential readers of the author's works, these analytical pieces give a good idea of what the author does well. Living authors are invited to make comments about their own work, and these add to the richness of the articles. All titles by an author are listed, including those written under pseudonyms. Novels containing a series character are also indicated.

Each preface in this series provides an overview of the specific genre and a reading list of books and articles about the genre. Genres are rather broadly defined. For instance, an article about the body of Mark Twain's work appears in *St. James Guide to Science Fiction Writers*, and P. D. James is included in both *Contemporary Novelists* and *St. James Guide to Crime and Mystery Writers*, in articles written by two different critics.

Reading the descriptive entries is useful whether we know the author's work or not, because doing so helps distinguish the elements of an author's style and the appeal the novelist has to the reader. The articles in the *St. James Guide* series seem to put into words just what we wish we had said to describe the tone and features of a title or author. We read about an author not only to confirm and validate our opinions about that author but also because the descriptions often make us aware of the same characteristics in other authors. This excerpt from the article on Jayne Ann Krentz, found in *Twentieth-Century Romance and Historical Writers*, not only suggests fellow writers of Contemporary Romances Nora Roberts and Susan Elizabeth Phillips, but it may also remind readers of the characters in Elizabeth Peters's Mystery series and lead interested readers to that genre as well.

> Krentz's heroines are unusually strong and determined. They also display a healthy sense of self-worth. . . . Krentz always presents a romance with sparks between the hero and heroine, snappy dialogue, vividly drawn characters and lots of humour thrown in.[9]

If your budget can accommodate these reference books, this series is a worthwhile addition to any readers' advisory reference shelf. These titles provide a good starting place when we want to learn more about authors. One of the joys of using these books is settling down to an extended session of reading the descriptions of various known and unknown authors, following leads from one author to another, and creating chains of similar authors. This activity can provide us with an overview of the various authors, as well as some idea of the appeal of genre and subgenres. It is useful to peruse previous editions as well, because authors may be profiled by different critics. Also, be aware that *Contemporary Novelists* carries deceased novelists for only one edition after their death.

Another series that demonstrates the type of reference work particularly useful for readers' advisory reference is Gale's *What Do I Read Next?*[10] Begun in 1990, this series highlights the year's publications in the Horror, Science Fiction, Fantasy, Romance, Mystery, and Western genres. Each section is written by a genre expert, and the introductory essays to each genre section highlight trends in the genre from the previous year. Within each section, entries provide the following information: author, title, subgenre, names of important characters, time period, locale, a brief plot summary, review citations, a list of selected titles by that author, and a list of similar authors and titles recommended for readers who enjoyed each book. As we mentioned earlier, good indexes are invaluable in readers' advisory reference books. This volume has a wide range of useful indexes, accessing Series, Time Period, Locale, Genre (with subgenres), Character Name, Character Descriptor (e.g., librarian), Author, and Title. Gale also offers an electronic version of this source, described in the next section.

A final reference source worthy of individual note is *To Be Continued,* by Merle Jacob and Hope Apple.[11] This annotated guide to books in thirteen hundred series includes both mainstream and genre fiction (although, unfortunately, not Mysteries). The excellent annotations, made accessible through Title, Genre, Subject and Literary Form, and Time and Place indexes, make this reference useful in helping readers to identify series of interest. (Not to mention the fact that the source is a real pleasure to explore in order to expand our own reading.) *To Be Continued* is also available electronically as part of Carl Corporation's *NoveList.*

You will undoubtedly find other useful resource books, many of them perhaps sitting right on your shelves. In addition to including the indexes and features discussed above, the best resources are put together by writers and compilers who love books and who want to pass that love and enjoyment on to others. When you find a good source, treasure it, for it will delight readers in your library and prove a useful tool in answering readers' advisory reference questions. And do, please, send us the title.

Electronic Sources

Electronic access to reference sources is growing in the field of readers' advisory. At this time there are two sources in the library market which provide the kind of information readers' advisors seek. As noted earlier, Gale's *What Do I Read Next?* has been published in book form since 1990. In 1996 an electronic version, including the data from all editions of the book version, was introduced on CD-ROM. This version includes access to material for children and young adults, as well as for adults. In addition, Gale has begun to expand the scope of this resource beyond the basic genres covered in the book version (Horror, Science Fiction, Fantasy, Romance, Mystery, and Westerns) to include Historical and Mainstream fiction as well. Award winners, best-sellers, and pathfinders, the latter provided by major public libraries, are also accessible and link users to full title entries. As in the book version, lists of similar and recommended authors are also retrievable.

Carl Corporation's *NoveList,* developed by readers' advisor Duncan Smith, has been available since 1994.[12] Data on adult, children's, and young adult titles from Hennepin County Public Library in Minnesota form the basis of this resource. *Booklist* reviews serve as the main source of annotations, but *NoveList* also includes annotations and index information from *Anatomy of Wonder 4: A Critical Guide to Science Fiction, Genreflecting,* and *To Be Continued.*[13] Extensive subject headings, including a range that exceeds those offered in *Fiction Catalog,* have been supplied by Hennepin County Public Library in Minnesota. A separate section lists award winners and links these titles to full descriptions in the *NoveList* data base. A matching feature allows users to find similar authors and titles and to explore subjects of interest.

Although electronic resources are certainly intriguing and useful, like their book counterparts, they are tools, or as *NoveList*'s Duncan Smith likes to say, they provide the staff with added memory.[14] They free staff from the difficulty of desperately trying to remember every author and title. They allow us to be facilitators—to act as guides to the collection—by expanding our memories and knowledge of popular fiction and by helping us retrieve information readily. Like other reference sources, they can be helpful memory-joggers, places to go when our minds go blank. They do not replace staff; they simply give us an added edge and another resource to use in working with patrons. Both of these electronic resources are rapidly changing and expanding; librarians interested in exploring electronic access should consult the publishers for up-to-date information.

The Internet is also becoming an important resource for readers' advisors. Since 1995, Fiction-L, a readers' advisory listserv developed and maintained by Roberta Johnson of the Morton Grove Public Library in Illinois, has provided a forum for information on readers' advisory tools and techniques as well as a place to post questions for its approximately eight hundred subscribers.[15] Readers' advisors from across the country, and indeed the world, post queries from staff and patrons. Very few librarians, seeking a particular author or title when a patron has offered only a sketchy description, fail to receive an answer from colleagues. Questions about similar authors are common, as are requests for lists of titles on a particular subject or ideas for displays or book lists. A comment from one reader inspires another librarian, and enthusiastic responses fill the list. The success of this resource underscores the cooperative nature of readers' advisory and reinforces that, although an individual cannot read everything, someone else may have read just what we are looking for, and we are all willing to share the fruits of our reading and knowledge. Many satisfied patrons and librarians have benefited from this and other on-line resources. The range of listservs, usenets, and Websites expands and changes daily, and interested readers' advisors should consult published sources on book-related sites, as well as use standard search engines.[16]

Readers' advisors need reference resources, if possible in both book and electronic formats. If nothing else, these sources help establish in the minds of patrons, and sometimes administrators, the fact that questions about fiction reading are legitimate and important, and that published resources exist to help answer such questions. We need to collect these memory-enhancing tools, not only to legitimatize our work but also to make research into unfamiliar authors, genres, and subjects more practical and rewarding. On the other hand, resources alone will never replace the human readers' advisor. Books and electronic sources will never be able to interpret the quirk of the eyebrow or other body language we learn to recognize and respond to as we talk with patrons about books. Resources provide that added memory for readers' advisors, and, if we make them readily available, they are often successfully and enjoyably used by patrons on their own.

Popular Fiction List

Although many librarians read genre fiction, it is the rare librarian indeed who has time to read extensively and can advise knowledgeably in all the genres patrons request. That is why we have found it useful to develop a list of genres, including representative authors, that are popular at our library. This kind of home-grown reference tool is an excellent supplement to reference books. It pulls together basic and frequently requested information into an easy-to-use resource that helps staff as they are expanding their own understanding of genre fiction and as they work with patrons. Such a list also does double duty by serving as a reading plan for readers' advisors, as we discuss in chapter 5.

It may be easiest to illustrate the value of having a list of popular genres and authors by describing the Popular Fiction List we created. The copy included in the Appendix is the winter 1997 version of our list, which was initially developed in 1983. Originally, our list consisted of twelve genres with twelve authors in each. Twelve is by no means a magic number, so choose a number you are comfortable with. In fact, in our latest version we have expanded the Popular Fiction List to thirteen genres, a baker's dozen. Before you decide how many and which authors to include, you may wish to read the section on Designing a Reading Plan in chapter 5, which explores the list's role as a training tool and reading plan. The decision to use the list in this way may affect which genres and how many authors you include. No matter what you decide, we recommend that some standard genres at least be included: Fantasy, Horror, Mystery/ Detective, Romance, Science Fiction, and Thriller. The others you choose should be based on your needs, situation, clientele, and collection.

Over time, our list has undergone many changes in both genres and authors included. For example, the first version had separate classifications for Historical Fiction and Family Saga, but we later combined them and finally eliminated Saga completely, as interest in sagas among both readers and publishers declined. When we met to discuss the most recent version of our list, we expanded it to thirteen genres with the addition of Women's Lives and Relationships. This was not a step that we took lightly. Over the past several years, we have experienced a growing interest, among both male and female readers, in novels by women that explore women's lives and their relationships. We first met the need through several very successful annotated book lists, but we finally decided to add this group of authors as a separate genre. Novels by these authors feature a female protagonist and usually follow only one main character. They focus on relationships—with family, friends, and lovers—and portray women trying to make sense of their lives. A range of popular authors, such as Danielle Steel, Barbara Delinsky, and Barbara Kingsolver, exemplify these characteristics.

The Modern Storyteller genre was a new addition to the second edition of our list, and we confess that this, too, is a grouping of our own invention. We developed this category based on conversations with readers who said they enjoy blockbuster novels—best-sellers with multiple plot lines and elements from several genres (often Thriller, Romance, and Mystery) combined into one big book. Subsequent conversations with readers have validated our belief that this is an identifiable group of authors who share the same appeal. As we continued exploring genres, we discovered that the stories they told were not necessarily "modern," so the category is now Storyteller and includes such authors as Ken Follett and John Grisham.

The Gentle Reads category may also require explanation. These authors write novels that contain no explicit sex or violence and that endorse traditional values. Many readers describe just this kind of book to us, and we find it very useful to have a list of authors we can suggest without hesitation or reservation. Gentle Reads, more than any other genre group on the list, present difficulties for staff and patrons alike. Classic author Miss Read may be the traditional benchmark, but some readers of this genre find her too gentle; they may prefer an author such as Eva Ibbotson, who takes them outside the quiet village setting but still evokes the same gentle "feel." Because these authors are difficult to find, we have expanded the scope to include Mystery writers as well. (These are indicated with an M on the list in the Appendix.) Although fiction published by Christian publishing houses would certainly fit here, it is not what every reader of this genre seeks, so we have included only representative authors.

Another nonstandard category we include is Literary Fiction. Originally called In a Class by Themselves, and then Literate Fiction, this group of authors writes complex, literate, multilayered novels that wrestle with universal dilemmas. That pattern is evident in the works of all the authors on our list, from Pat Conroy to Alice Hoffman. These are the authors we often suggest to readers who seek award-winning writers.

Crime/Caper first appeared on the 1993 version of our list. These writers—Carl Hiaasen, Michael Connelly, and Elmore Leonard, for example—share elements with many authors on the Mystery and Suspense genre lists but are not necessarily writers of those genres. Social and moral issues are frequently the themes of these authors; in addition, criminal investigation, hard-edged details of crimes, flawed heroes, and a darker tone, sometimes accompanied by black humor, characterize these popular authors and their books.

The Romance genre has been expanded to include writers we call Romantic Storyteller authors, who often write larger books that include Storyteller elements from other genres, such as Mystery or Suspense. Nora Roberts is an example of such an author; although she does write straight Romances, she also writes bigger books which include Suspense, Mystery, and Adventure elements.

While it is important to include genres popular in your library, these should be true, definable genres, in which specific elements characterize the pattern followed by the books. In developing a list of popular genres, there is always the temptation to create genres from groups of authors who are really linked in other ways, perhaps by subject or even gender, rather than genre. African-American authors, for example, do not constitute a separate genre, since books by these authors are not written to a particular, identifiable pattern, as genre fiction always is by definition. Pulitzer Prize winner Toni Morrison and Mystery writer Eleanor Taylor Bland are both African-American writers, but each has her own following of fans and their books differ dramatically. If Bland or other African-American Mystery writers are popular, they belong on the Mystery genre list, not on a separate list that merely groups authors by race or gender. Creating a book list that reflects the range of African-American authors is a better way to meet interest and demand for books by these authors.

In some ways, a Popular Fiction List really belongs with the reference books we cannot live without. While we can use a list someone else developed, it will not serve our staff and patrons as well as one we develop ourselves. Creating this kind of list as a departmental training exercise is discussed in chapter 7. You can certainly develop your own list from scratch, but it may be easier to start with our list, included in the Appendix, and tear it apart. Simply start with a genre you know to be popular in your library and consider each of the authors, deleting those not popular and adding others that are, following the suggestions detailed below. You will notice that the list in the Appendix consists only of genres and authors, not titles. Discovering typical titles by each author is part of the training process as we develop a reading plan based on genres and authors on this list.

The first step in constructing your own list is to choose genres that reflect the interests of your readers and the authors available in your collection. As we mentioned above, there are several traditional genres that we feel any such list should include; but any additional choices—which genres and how many additional genres— should reflect your library's situation. Not every community needs Crime/Caper or Gentle Reads, for instance, but there is bound to be something special that your readers request and with which you and your staff need to be familiar.

In creating any list of popular fiction, we need to do some preliminary information gathering. The first step is to determine which genres and authors our library patrons are reading. Several simple survey techniques may be used to give an indication of fiction reading patterns. You might try keeping track of all your readers' advisory interactions for a few months. We simply kept a sheet of paper at our service desk and indicated any author or genre that was specifically requested by a patron. By examining the list at the end of that period, we could see which genres and authors were in demand. Additionally, surveying the staff that works with fiction readers, perhaps asking them which frequently requested authors seem to be too popular ever to be found on the shelves, is another way to identify authors and genres that have been popular among readers. Circulation staff can often identify authors and genres that circulate heavily. Shelvers are often an overlooked source of information; if they are assigned to shelve particular sections of the alphabet or individual genre sections, they have a good sense of which authors they shelve most frequently. By surveying the books that are returned and noting those that are put on reserve, we can obtain even more information. These informal surveys should provide enough information to use in choosing which genres and authors to include in a Popular Fiction List.

More formal and time-consuming methods of obtaining information also exist. A carefully conducted reader survey, using a well-thought-out questionnaire, would certainly furnish useful data and would undoubtedly add to the findings obtained from the more informal sources. Weeding the fiction collection is another activity that can provide useful information about patrons' reading habits. A very good indication of our readers' tastes may be obtained by checking circulation figures during weeding and noting the authors who have gone out both frequently and recently. As we all know, weeding is also an excellent way to acquaint the readers' advisory staff with the collection in general and with specific authors and titles that are popular in our libraries. (As any librarian also knows, however, large-scale weeding is a major undertaking that involves time and money and should not be embarked upon lightly.)

Next, we need to select representative authors from our collections within each genre we choose. In addition to the survey techniques described above, we might also search reference books and reviews to find key authors in a genre. Here are some simple guidelines to follow in choosing authors to include.

1. The authors need to have written more than one or two books in the genre. We strongly discourage including an author who has written only a few books. If we include such an author, we limit the usefulness of our list. For example, because of Colleen McCullough's extremely popular book *The Thorn Birds,* readers think of her as a writer of Family Sagas; in fact, this is the only saga she has written to date, and she is therefore not a good choice for inclusion if Family Saga is one of your genres.
2. Several titles by each author should be available in our collection. It is no help if an author has written twenty books but our library has only one or two of them. Interlibrary loan is a possible source for additional titles once we have hooked a reader; but as much as possible, this list should provide instant gratification. Books should be immediately available for readers whenever they are in the library.
3. To be useful, the Popular Fiction List should not be just a specialist's idea of the "best" in a genre. Originally our list included both classic and popular authors. Recently, as a training exercise, we sought to change that emphasis and include only the most popular authors with our readers. Our concern was that it was too easy to fill the list with classic authors that no one, except perhaps students completing assignments, reads anymore. While our list now reflects popular authors more accurately, it must be supplemented with classic authors when we use it to gain background in a genre. For example, when we

began our study of the Mystery genre, we felt we needed to review classic authors as well as currently popular ones. In our early reading we paired Agatha Christie with Robert Barnard, Dorothy L. Sayers with P. D. James, and classic Private Investigator mysteries by Raymond Chandler and Dashiell Hammett with those of Robert B. Parker. If your list, like ours, emphasizes currently popular authors, you will need to devise ways to gain familiarity with classic authors as well in order to understand a genre.

4. In compiling our lists, we strive for a balanced grouping of authors and try to include those who represent diverse aspects of the genres we know to be popular among our readers. Our Mystery/Detective list, for example, would not be as useful if it included only writers of Police Procedurals.

5. Be careful of authors who write in more than one genre. Unless our collections are physically divided by genres to some extent, a reader tracking down an author of Thrillers may pick up the same author's Mysteries or Westerns by mistake and be disappointed, not to mention confused. Include such authors if you feel they are too important to overlook, but caution users of your list that the authors write in more than one genre.

Not every popular author can necessarily be slotted into a genre on this list. If several very popular authors seem not to fit, they should be considered carefully to see if they share elements that make them a genre of their own. In many ways, our Storyteller genre started as a catchall for authors who did not seem to fit into the standard genres; further reading and discussion revealed a similar pattern in these books, and we were able to designate them as a separate genre.

You may, as we do, get questions about your list, such as, Why is this prominent author not included? The answer may be that you simply did not think of him or her. However, it is also possible that you would not include an author that someone else suggests just because that author is not popular in your library. The point of the list is to include a range of authors that our patrons enjoy reading, not authors we think they *ought* to read.

One last word: The popularity of the individual genres on this list can give us an idea of genres for which there is a ready-made audience for annotated book lists. The two projects complement each other. The genre lists give us a start with a core group of possible authors, while our work on the book list may uncover authors who deserve inclusion in this core list. The popularity of and demand for Legal Thrillers, for example, would likely be better met by an annotated book list, which reflects the range of this subgenre, than by a list of authors on a Popular Fiction List, which readers are not as likely to see and use.

One last caution: Do not aim for the ultimate list; it is better to have a partial list, even if it is just in draft form and not available for patron perusal, than to strive for the perfect resource. Expect to revise the list regularly to reflect your own expanding knowledge of popular fiction as well as changes in your patrons' reading tastes. Since this list can be an important reference tool, do not let your thinking about a genre progress too far beyond your list; update it regularly to keep the list current and useful.

Although you will not want to think about updating the list before you have written a first draft, updating the reading list by reevaluating both the genres and the authors included is another important activity. Ours has changed dramatically since its creation in 1983, with genres and authors added and deleted to reflect changes in reading interests at our library. Readers' advisors can discuss which authors are still being requested and should stay on the list, which should be deleted, and which newly popular authors should be added. (*Note:* Once you have set a comfortable number of authors within a genre, it is best to hold to that number. It is easy to keep adding new authors without deleting others, but adhering to a set number makes you more conscious of which authors really belong on the list. If you need a longer list of authors in a genre, you may want to do a book list instead of expanding this list.)

The Popular Fiction List became a lifeline for us and our staff when we first started working closely with fiction readers. We developed it, quite simply, out of desperation. Early on we found that the simple fact that we had a list of popular authors to refer to and share with readers made us much more comfortable in talking with readers about genres. If the patrons said they read Romances, we had a list readily available of possible authors to suggest, even though the range of subgenres included meant that not all Romance readers would necessarily enjoy all the authors. Still, it was a list to hold in hand, to give us some measure of confidence as we began working with readers. The list's manageable size also meant that when a patron mentioned a name we knew to be on the list, we could usually place it in a genre and mention other authors in that genre. Since the list contained only authors whose books we owned, we were likely to find books on the shelf for the patron. The psychological benefit of having a list of names, classified by genre, to share with readers is impossible to calculate. We worried a lot less about drawing a blank and not being able to find any books to give patrons because, if all else failed, we always had the Popular Fiction List as a backup source of 144 popular authors. In addition, because we knew these to be popular authors at our library, this list has always provided a supplemental source when the patron just wanted a good read. With the list, we had popular authors we could start talking about.

A Popular Fiction List, then, can be an important readers' advisory resource. It can help give staff confidence in talking with readers about a genre, as well as providing a reading list of popular and representative authors. A well-constructed list can be a valuable guide to help readers' advisory staff become more familiar with popular genres. We discuss this feature more fully in chapter 5 in the section on Designing a Reading Plan.

Staff as a Resource

Readers' advisors rely extensively on staff and staff-created resources. In chapter 6, we discuss the bookmarks and annotated book lists that staff create. These become useful reference tools for all staff, not just those who write them; in addition, they become resources—guides to aspects of the collection—for patrons as well.

The Popular Fiction List is another source that, once created, allows staff to become a resource and share their knowledge of particular authors and/or specific genres. This list of popular fiction should be posted in the readers' advisory staff area, and all advisors should develop the habit of initialing authors' names as they read. Knowing which readers' advisor is well read in a particular area alerts staff to a resource person whom they may consult when they want to increase their own knowledge of a particular genre or when they have a patron who wants to talk with another fan. An initialed list also serves as a gauge that indicates how staff individually, and the readers' advisory staff in general, are growing in their knowledge of popular genre authors.

Finally, readers' advisory staff should remember that all library staff, including those who do not specifically do readers' advisory, can be excellent resources. All readers who are willing to share information on the books they have read or heard about add to our store of knowledge about books—and readers. In this era of straitened circumstances, with its emphasis on expensive electronic access to materials and information, it is easy to forget that one of our most useful reference sources is the knowledge of our staff. Readers' advisors are readers who enjoy sharing their knowledge and love of books—with fellow staff members and patrons alike. Conversations about books, sharing knowledge of what we are reading, is one of the easiest ways to tap this resource. Strategies and techniques throughout this book rely on the communal nature of readers' advisory and sharing, both informally through conversation and more formally through annotations and book lists. Readers' advisory work is about making connections—among authors and their books, among readers and staff and the books they share, and with colleagues and all who read and share their pleasure in the books they enjoy. Sharing information is the linchpin of readers' advisory work, and we all need to work on ways to do this consistently and effectively. We talk more of sharing information in chapter 7 on training but it is too important—and too often neglected—not to be emphasized here as well.

Reference sources are the backbone of a readers' advisory department. It is therefore important for librarians to understand what elements make reference sources specifically useful for readers' advisory work and to familiarize ourselves with the materials we now own, as well as to purchase and/or develop others to enhance our resources.

Reference sources—paper, electronic, and human—are a good starting point for both new and experienced readers' advisors. These resources provide information that readers' advisors can use to become familiar with authors, titles, and types of fiction. Thus, they are important both as reference tools for answering questions and as training materials. Making readers' advisory reference sources available and using them with patrons validate the readers' advisory requests patrons make and emphasize the fact that we are treating these questions as seriously as any other reference question. Reference sources are only one facet of readers' advisory, one type of tool we can become familiar with and rely on. In the next chapter, we consider in detail the nature of a book's appeal, how readers' advisors identify this elusive quality, and how we use it in working with readers.

Notes

1. *Fiction Catalog,* 13th ed. (New York: H. W. Wilson, 1996).
2. Diana Tixier Herald, *Genreflecting: A Guide to Reading Interests in Genre Fiction,* 4th ed. (Englewood, Colo.: Libraries Unlimited, 1995).

3. Ibid., xviii.

4. Ibid., xxvi.

5. Janet Husband and Jonathan F. Husband, *Sequels: An Annotated Guide to Novels in Series,* 3rd ed. (Chicago: American Library Assn., 1997).

6. Readers' Advisory Committee, "Readers' Advisory Reference Tools."

7. Aruna Vasudevan, ed., *Twentieth-Century Romance and Historical Writers,* 3rd ed. (Detroit: St. James, 1994); Jay P. Pederson, ed., *St. James Guide to Crime and Mystery Writers,* 4th ed. (Detroit: St. James, 1996); David Pringle, ed., *St. James Guide to Fantasy Writers* (Detroit: St. James, 1996.); Jay P. Pederson, ed., *St. James Guide to Science Fiction Writers,* 4th ed. (Detroit: St. James, 1996); Geoff Sadler, ed., *Twentieth-Century Western Writers,* 2nd ed. (Detroit: St. James, 1991).

8. Susan Windisch Brown, ed., *Contemporary Novelists,* 6th ed. (Detroit: St. James, 1996).

9. Barbara E. Kemp, "Krentz, Jayne Ann," in Aruna Vasudevan, ed., *Twentieth-Century Romance and Historical Writers,* 3rd ed. (Detroit: St. James, 1994), 375.

10. Barron et al., eds., *What Do I Read Next 1996: A Reader's Guide to Current Genre Fiction* (Detroit: Gale, 1996).

11. Merle L. Jacob and Hope Apple, *To Be Continued: An Annotated Guide to Sequels* (Phoenix: Oryx, 1995).

12. *NoveList* CD-ROM, Carl Corporation, Denver, Colo., 1994.

13. Neil Barron, ed., *Anatomy of Wonder 4: A Critical Guide to Science Fiction* (New Providence, N.J.: Bowker, 1995).

14. Duncan Smith, "Readers' Advisory Goes Electronic" (paper presented at Public Library Association Sixth National Conference, March 26–30, 1996).

15. Fiction-L [electronic bulletin board]. Available from majordomo@list-serv.nslsilus.org.

16. For example, Evan Morris, *The Book Lover's Guide to the Internet* (New York: Columbine, 1996). See also Robert Burgin, "Appendix 1: Readers' Advisory Resources for Adults on the Internet," in *Guiding the Reader to the Next Book,* 185–96.

3 Articulating a Book's Appeal

When we began reading popular fiction, writing annotations, and talking with fiction readers, we saw that some books seemed to fit together—seemed to appeal to the same readers—and we became more and more interested in discovering the reason why this was so. In this chapter we want to address more specifically the issue of how we connect different books and actually ascertain an individual book's appeal. We will examine step-by-step the crucial elements that help us define and describe a book's appeal—pacing, characterization, story line, and frame—and discuss how a readers' advisor looks at books to discover their appeal. First, however, we need to discuss why this way of thinking about books is so important in readers' advisory work.

From the beginning of our work with fiction readers, we saw that an understanding of appeal is the keystone of successful readers' advisory work. Years of working with fiction readers and training readers' advisors have confirmed this early experience. We have found that most readers are usually not looking for a book on a certain subject. They want a book with a particular "feel." As we work with readers in libraries, it very quickly becomes clear that we need to understand both subject headings and appeal characteristics if we really want to serve readers. In the last chapter, we highlighted the importance of discovering reference resources that provide subject access to fiction. However, these reference tools do not address appeal, the feel of a book, and its effect on readers.

What exactly do we mean when we talk about appeal, and how do appeal elements differ from subject headings? Our meaning may be clearer if we answer the second question first. Consider the different ways we might describe a book: by basic plot, subject descriptors, and then appeal. In *One True Thing*, Anna Quindlen writes of a young woman working out her relationship with her parents during the months when her mother is dying of cancer.[1] Subject headings on Carl Corporation's *NoveList* include the following: FATHER AND DAUGHTER, MOTHER AND DAUGHTER, EUTHANASIA, and WOMEN CANCER PATIENTS.[2] When we consider the way in which this book appeals to readers, however, we think in terms of pacing, characterization, story line, and atmosphere. We add to this skeleton the sense that the story unfolds at a leisurely pace and establishes an emotional bond with the reader. The book draws the reader in with its sympathetic portrayal of characters and the intimate, introspective view of the protagonist, the daughter, as we are privy to her thoughts as well as her actions. Readers may also be attracted by the moral and social issues raised by this thought-provoking story, the interrelated characters, the heartwarming tone, and the ultimately satisfying resolution.

Unless readers are actively seeking titles within given subject headings, they will likely be able to make better use of the appeal elements in deciding whether this is a novel for them. We do, of course, find readers seeking novels on euthanasia or cancer patients or mother-daughter relationships, but the subject headings alone give no indication of the tone of a novel or of the manner in which its author handles these subjects. Appeal elements describe more accurately the "feel" of a book. Appeal elements take us beyond the bare bones provided by subject descriptors and reveal more of the novel's essence.

If we consider how we interact with readers when we talk about books, we realize immediately that we are far more likely to share a book in terms of its appeal than in terms of its plot or the subject headings assigned it. We may talk about the black humor in Carl Hiaasen's offbeat crime novels set in southern Florida or the elegant, evocative prose that characterizes Michael Dorris's work. While subject headings may address aspects of these descriptive elements, they cannot convey the same depth of meaning. Appeal is what takes us—and readers—beyond mere subjects and plot lines. As we will see in this chapter, appeal terms open up a book for readers and allow them to decide if this is a book they are in the mood to read and might enjoy. Thinking and talking in terms of appeal simply provides a formal structure to the way we naturally think about and describe books.

Now back to the first question: What exactly do we mean by appeal? The elements in books that make patrons enjoy them constitute the appeal of a book for the reader. That sounds straightforward and, in fact, readers and readers' advisors often recognize this appeal long before we can actually define it. As we can see from the above description of Quindlen's book, we are far more likely to think about a book in terms of its appeal than we are in terms of a plot description. As readers, as well as readers' advisors, we often develop a sixth sense about which books go together and interest the same readers—not necessarily because the books are in the same genre or deal with the same subject, but because they evoke the same responses; they have the same "feel."

The problem for readers' advisors becomes one of more consistently identifying this "feel" so that we can work better with readers. While appeal may be the key to identifying what a reader enjoyed in one book and may be looking for in another, putting this appeal into words can be a challenge. Although difficult, the process of articulating appeal is not impossible since we naturally describe books by appeal—by the way they affect us—whether we are conscious of this or not.

Calling a book a page-turner or a compelling read identifies a book's *pacing*. Comments about quirky characters or about introspective, involving first-person novels refer to *characterization* and how it affects readers. Whenever we describe a book's plot as complex or convoluted, as employing multiple plot lines, or as dealing with moral or social issues from child abuse to politics, we are reflecting *story line* elements that describe a book's appeal to readers. Referring to the wealth of historical detail or the interesting pieces of information about antique clothing suggests the author's attention to background detail, just as the use of adjectives like *bleak* or *upbeat* suggests a particular atmosphere or tone, and all of these are part of the *frame* an author constructs. These are the kinds of terms we use daily in describing books, without thinking that we are doing anything out of the ordinary. We are speaking as readers in the language other readers understand.

In this chapter, we plan to help crystallize this descriptive process. We want to formalize the way we naturally think about books so that it becomes easier to recognize appeal more consistently and to describe books in terms that allow readers to decide if certain titles will meet their needs. These techniques can be applied not only to books we have read but also to those books we have only read about or heard of. What we suggest here is simply a more systematic approach that capitalizes on a reader's natural inclinations in describing books to fellow readers. Our discussion of how to make this part of our routine is centered around the four basic elements—pacing, characterization, story line, and frame—which, singly and in combination, seem to address the ways in which books affect readers. We will consider each appeal element separately, focusing on both the language we use to share that appeal with readers and a list of possible questions we can consider in identifying that appeal. Although the list may seem overwhelming at first, it is really simply a compilation of memory-joggers, an incomplete catalog of the ways we already think about and describe books. In our library, we use this kind of question list when we are making notes about books we have read, an activity we discuss in detail in chapter 5.

In the discussion of each element, notice that readers' advisors do not measure books by literary and critical standards, but by readers' perceptions. While it is important for readers' advisors to be aware of levels of writing styles, well-developed characters, and consistent plots so that we can suggest the best books we know, readers' advisors should also be aware that readers themselves often tolerate a wide range of quality if other elements of appeal are present.

Pacing

Pacing is the first element readers are aware of, albeit often unconsciously. If we talk with readers about a book's pacing, we might say it is fast-paced, or a page-turner, or that the story unfolds at a more leisurely pace. The book may be densely written, which promises a more measured pace. Or we might describe it as engrossing, a book so involving we do not want to put it down. How do we discover this information? What clues do we as readers find in the books to help us identify pacing, and how do we translate our reactions into a vocabulary to use with readers? Figure 3.1 summarizes the questions we might ask to determine a book's pacing.

Are characters and plot quickly revealed or slowly unveiled?

How does the author move the reader along—by quickly revealing characters and actions or by slowly unveiling the book's plot and

Figure 3.1
Questions to Consider to Identify Pacing

1. Are characters and plot quickly revealed or slowly unveiled?
2. Is there more dialogue or description?
3. Is the book densely written?
4. Are there short sentences, short paragraphs, and short chapters?
5. Are there multiple plot lines, flashbacks, alternating chapters related from different points of view; or is there a straight-line plot?
6. Do characters act or react to events?
7. Is the book end oriented or open ended?
8. What is the pattern of the pacing?

purpose? Do readers fall right into the action of the book, or does the story move at a more measured pace? When we were first offering readers' advisory at our library, we were desperately searching for more authors who wrote like Mary Higgins Clark, who was not writing quickly enough to satisfy her many fans. We came across Ruth Rendell, who also wrote fairly short novels of psychological suspense, often featuring women in danger. When we offered Rendell to a Clark fan, we were told in no uncertain terms that Rendell did not share the same appeal. After some discussion, we discovered that pacing made the difference between the two; Rendell's book simply did not move at the same quick pace as Clark's.

Readers often will relate to this difference and prefer to read one type of book over the other. It is interesting to note that readers' preferences for one style or the other may not be something they can define, and if they are faced with a choice between a "fast-paced" or "slow-paced" book, readers will almost always choose the former. Slow pacing seems to have negative connotations. However, if each book is described invitingly, readers can more readily make choices about what they would really like to read. In the readers' advisory interview, we may offer two books in order to determine the type of pacing the reader is in the mood for at the moment. We may describe one novel as featuring nonstop action, with many plot twists, and the other book as developing more slowly, with characters and story line unfolding as the book progresses. Given options such as these, readers can choose the type of pacing they are in the mood to read.

Is there more dialogue or description?

Dialogue often moves the reader along more quickly, while description tends to slow the flow of the novel. Readers' advisors can usually tell if one or the other predominates simply by flipping through the book. More white space on the page generally means there is more dialogue and the book can likely be read more quickly. To see this difference, riffle through the pages to compare Amanda Quick's racy Regency Romances, which feature snappy dialogue and a page-turning flow, to Sharyn McCrumb's ballad series, Mysteries in which evocative descriptions of characters and place draw the reader in and purposefully slow the pace.

Is the book densely written?

Density suggests elegance, but it also reflects the amount of detail and description an author employs. Densely written books, in which the language is emphasized and each word is important, do not flow in the same way as books written in a more conversational style. The former may be more lyrical or poetic, and readers may choose this type of novel because they take pleasure in concentrating on the prose, the beauty of the language. This is not to say that some fast-paced books are not densely, elegantly written, but faster pacing usually demands a less dense style. Denser, more lyrical writing usually slows the pacing, as it requires readers to concentrate on words as well as characters and story, even when there is a lot of dialogue. Minette Walters' award-winning Mysteries are a good example. In contrast, a more conversational—or even cinematic—style, such as that used by Clive Cussler in his Dirk Pitt Adventure novels, utilizes free-flowing prose that directs readers to follow action and characters, rather than to read each word closely for depth of meaning. Densely written books may be fast-paced, but they usually build in intensity and do not necessarily seem fast at first. Thomas Harris's classic novel of serial murder, *The Silence of the Lambs,* is a good example of a densely written book that keeps the reader turning the pages at a fast pace.[3]

Are there short sentences, short paragraphs, and short chapters?

These also affect the flow of the novel, as they pull the reader more quickly through the story. Longer sentences, paragraphs, and chapters often reflect denser prose, usually more description, and thus slower pacing. Robert B. Parker's Spenser Mysteries exemplify the former type, while P. D. James's style, featuring longer passages, is an example of the second. These questions can be answered easily by physically glancing at the book; we can often offer these useful observations about pacing to patrons even when we are unfamiliar with the books in question, simply by riffling through the books.

Are there multiple plot lines, flashbacks, or alternating chapters related from different points of view; or is there a straight-line plot?

Each type of plot line can be used to speed or slow the pacing. In Mystery and Suspense novels with multiple plot lines, each thread of the plot may contain a vital clue or piece of information. Even though readers may need to concentrate more to follow the threads and see how they ultimately intertwine, they may read more quickly—or perceive the book as faster paced—because of the alternating plot lines. On the other hand, this profusion of plot and character details may complicate, and thus slow, the story.

Changing points of view may have a similar effect. This technique may slow the story as it forces readers to reacquaint themselves with the characters each time they appear, but it may also speed the flow because readers want to know what is happening, especially if one chapter ends as a cliffhanger and then the next chapter features another character or plot line. Again, Thomas Harris's novels of serial murderers are a good example. In these, the story and the reader's focus alternate between detective and killer, but since chapters end with readers left on the edge of their seat, they read quickly to discover the outcome. This technique also allows more depth of characterization, however, and that may force a more leisurely pace. Whatever its effect on pacing, this approach has a particular appeal to readers who appreciate the insight it gives them into characters, and if we are aware of its presence in a book, we can share that information with readers.

Do characters act or react to events?

In some books, characters are reacting to events as they occur rather than being more involved physically in the action. In the former case, the pace is often slower, more involving, more intimate. Placing characters in physical jeopardy usually speeds the action and, thus, the pacing. For example, Ruth Rendell takes us inside the minds of her characters, and we relate to them as they consider their actions. In contrast, Mary Higgins Clark puts her characters in physical jeopardy and forces them to act, pulling us through the story more quickly.

Is the book end oriented or open ended?

Readers who ask for fast-paced books are often looking for novels that are end oriented, those which focus on how the plot will be worked out—on solving the mystery, rescuing the characters from danger, finding a mate. Slower-paced novels are often open ended, lacking total resolution. Many readers of these novels relish discovering what happens to the characters as events unfold; they relate to the characters' reactions rather than to the action, or perhaps to the working out of a particular concept or idea. Thus, if readers request other titles like Peter Høeg's haunting *Smilla's Sense of Snow,* it is useful to consider if the ambiguous ending is part of the appeal before offering something like Martin Cruz Smith's *Gorky Park,* which may seem similar on the surface in terms of frame and characterization, but which clearly provides its protagonist with a tenable resolution.[4]

What is the pattern of the pacing?

Does the book grip the reader immediately or build in intensity? Pacing is more than how quickly or slowly one reads the book or how the action progresses. There is also a pattern to pacing. Popular authors of the last century wrote according to a pattern that is in sharp contrast to that of many of today's best-selling authors. In most of Charles Dickens's novels, for example, the first one hundred pages are devoted primarily to introducing characters and setting up the story. Later the pacing increases dramatically, but the first section of the book moves slowly. Most best-selling authors today hook readers in the first few paragraphs with dramatic action, and this immediacy is the signature of these authors, just as the slower introduction is Dickens's usual signature.

Pacing, then, is determined by the reader's perception of a combination of factors, ranging from the amount of dialogue or description to the density of the writing, the way characters react, and the way the story is constructed. By understanding these elements and how they affect readers, readers' advisors can often pick out elements from conversations about a book, from reviews, or in our own reading to use in describing books to readers. It is clear, too, how thoroughly these appeal elements intertwine and overlap to give an overall impression of a book. This will become more evident in our discussion of the next element of appeal, characterization.

Characterization

How do an author's characterizations affect readers? One need only look to the Mystery genre to see how we relate to increasingly popular series characters, whose lives we follow through a succession of novels. We are also intrigued by eccentric or strong secondary characters, whose presence implies depth in the level of the book's characterizations. Some readers prefer introspective characters, and others favor books with several characters whose lives and activities intertwine. Still other readers describe themselves as looking for character-centered books. The following questions, summarized in Figure 3.2, aid in understanding the role of characterization in a book's appeal.

Figure 3.2
Questions to Consider to Identify Characterization

1. Are the characters developed over time, or are they stereotypes we recognize immediately?
2. Is the focus on a single character or on several whose lives are intertwined?
3. What is the point of view from which the story is told?
4. Is characterization the most important aspect of the book?
5. Is the reader expected to identify with the characters or observe them?
6. Are there series characters, followed through and developed over several related novels?
7. Are there memorable and important secondary characters?

Are the characters developed over time, or are they stereotypes we recognize immediately?

How does the author present the character? In Ed McBain's 87th Precinct Police Procedurals, for example, the reader recognizes and relates to the members of the police force from the very first pages. By using recognizable stereotypes, McBain can draw the reader quickly into the story. And, although the characters may change from book to book and even within a book, they remain readily identifiable—though not exaggerated—types. Other authors present characters who grow and change during the course of a novel. Anne Tyler's characters, in contrast to those of McBain, reveal their natures over time. We learn to know them only a little at a time and our vision keeps changing. Fans of this type of characterization, of unique and often surprising characters, are often displeased if we suggest novels in which the characters are not developed in the same way. Asking readers to describe characters they have enjoyed—or not enjoyed—usually makes it clear which type of characters they prefer.

Is the focus on a single character or on several characters whose lives are intertwined?

If there are several characters, how important are the relationships among them? Much genre fiction relies on a single main character who dominates the novel. In the Storyteller genre, however, multiple characters demand multiple, intertwining plot lines. In Elizabeth Adler's *The Rich Shall Inherit,* we meet each of the possible heirs one at a time and learn each one's story; later in the novel their lives intersect, and we see the relationships among them.[5]

What is the point of view from which the story is told?

First person narration is usually more intimate than third person, taking the reader inside the main character's thoughts. Many Private Investigator Mysteries are first person narrations, with the reader seeing all the protagonist sees and acting as a sounding board for the detective's mental conjectures. Sue Grafton's private investigator, Kinsey Millhone, is a good example of this point of view, and her mental ruminations add to our understanding of her character and her case. Historical fiction offers another example. There is an obvious difference between Robert Graves' *I, Claudius,* with its rather jumbled first-person account of actions and reactions, and Colleen McCullough's series covering the history of ancient Rome.[6] The latter employs third person and a straightforward, detail-laden historical explication of events. Both offer sound historical detail, but the difference in point of view creates two unique books. It is important to be aware of this difference because, in our experience, some readers react strongly to narrative voice, disliking the intimacy of first person.

Point of view is more than just narrative voice, however. More important, readers' advisors need to discover the answer to the question, Whose story is this? How is the point of view integral in shaping the story? Some genres are dependent on point of view. Romantic Suspense, according to our readers, has to be written from the threatened heroine's point of view, whether in first or third person, or the story simply does not have the same appeal for them. In many novels of serial murder, readers expect to get the point of view of both the killer and the detective. Seeing both points of view gives readers a sense of omniscience and the ability to perceive possible outcomes; they know who is evil and what he is planning, but they also have an idea when he will strike. This element separates these novels from Horror books, in which the reader does not always know the evil and expects to be jarred at irregular intervals as the unexpected occurs. For this reason, Horror novels do not appeal in the same way to readers who are fans of serial murder novels.

Is characterization the most important aspect of the book?

Are the characters more important than the plot, setting, or atmosphere? Readers often describe themselves as enjoying character-centered novels, by which they usually mean books in which characters—their actions, reactions, thoughts, and lives—are the most important element. The author's energy is directed primarily toward character development. Michael Shaara's *The Killer Angels,* which analyzes the Battle of Gettysburg through the eyes of its participants and reveals as much about the people as the battle, is a classic example.[7] Since character development and pacing usually work at odds with each other, books described as character centered are generally not perceived as fast-paced.

Is the reader expected to identify with the characters or observe them?

Are we drawn into the characters' stories or distanced from them, with the story told to the readers rather than experienced through the eyes of the characters? In the former case, readers receive a more intimate picture; in the latter, readers are more distanced from the characters. Are characters sympathetically or objectively portrayed? Some characters are meant to be sympathized with (Delderfield's Englishmen, for example), while others, those of Jane Smiley in *A Thousand Acres*, for instance, offer a more cerebral appeal, allowing the reader to observe, rather than participate in, their lives.[8]

Are there series characters, followed through and developed over several related novels?

Many readers enjoy series and look for all books in which a series character appears. The Mystery genre offers a wealth of series characters, many of whom readers follow for decades, becoming intimately involved in their lives and interests as well as in their cases. Other genres offer numerous examples, and even nongenre fiction has a place for series characters. Consider, for example, John Updike's Rabbit novels, each of which reflects a decade of contemporary life and opinions from the 1950s to the '80s.

Are there memorable and important secondary characters?

Since they may help define the tone and atmosphere of the book, secondary characters can be as important as the protagonists who define its viewpoint. Recurring secondary characters provide interesting plot lines that keep series fresh. They reveal information about the main characters from a different point of view. Many are so well developed and interesting in their own right that they attract readers who follow them as closely as the protagonist in a series. Where, for example, would Sherlock Holmes be without Dr. Watson or Nero Wolfe without Archie Goodwin? In fact, secondary characters can add to the overall appeal of a series or of a single title that features strong characterization. Both their role in the story and their interaction with the protagonist add an extra dimension to many works of fiction. Some readers also follow series for this pleasure in the range of well-developed secondary characters who appear regularly. Anne Perry's Great-aunt Vespasia in the Inspector and Charlotte Pitt Mysteries and Lady Callandra Daviot in the Monk Mystery series come immediately to mind. We try to watch for elements of personal appeal, ranging from the romantic to the zany, among protagonists and secondary characters, as these elements are often exactly what some readers tell us they are looking for; they add to the charm and appeal of a book as well.

While these may seem a lot of questions to be aware of in considering characterization, the answers to them are easily found in reviews, on book jackets, and in conversations with readers, as well as in the books we actually read. Fans can effortlessly describe the kinds of characters they enjoy, often more easily than they can remember or describe a plot. Simply asking a question such as, "Did it take you a while to know the characters, or did they seem familiar right away?" gives us quick insight into the nature of the characterization in a book a reader has read.

Story Line

When we think about story line and describe it to other readers, we go beyond mere plot summary. Books may be violent (John Sandford's novels of serial murder) or gentle (Jeanette Oke's prairie novels), issue oriented (Brian Aldiss's Science Fiction series set on Helliconia) or action oriented (Tom Clancy's Thrillers), or a combination of these. We describe books as family centered, inspirational, tragic, or racy, relying on a vocabulary designed to reflect the impact of the story line on the feel of the book. Figure 3.3 lists useful questions to ask readers.

Figure 3.3
Questions to Consider to Identify Story Line

1. Does the story emphasize people or situations and events?
2. What is the author's intention in regard to story line?
3. Is the focus of the story more interior and psychological or exterior and action oriented?

Does the story emphasize people or situations and events?

What is the author's treatment of the subject? In comparing two Espionage novels, for instance, we may note that one emphasizes political dilemmas, while the other concentrates on the lives of the characters caught up in the drama. Adam Hall's Quiller, who remains a distant figure in the series of Thrillers in which he stars, contrasts sharply with Dorothy Gilman's Mrs. Pollifax, who rivals Miss Marple in her skill at extracting personal information from those with whom she comes into contact. When the plots of actual books are described from this standpoint, readers often realize that they are more interested in one aspect than the other.

What is the author's intention in regard to story line?

Is this serious drama or soap opera, or is it a little of both? Both Elizabeth Berg and Danielle Steel write about women and the problems they face in their lives. While both deal with serious issues, they treat them very differently, and it is unlikely that Steel readers would appreciate Berg's weightier approach or that Berg's fans would find Steel's treatment satisfactory. Is the author's intent comedy or satire, or is it to take a more serious look at a moral or social issue? While writers such as James W. Hall and Edward Abbey may deal with serious issues, their satiric approaches to those issues are dramatically different from that of Sue Miller, who has a more serious bent. Each type of writing has a particular appeal and a loyal audience, so it is important to recognize the differences between them.

Is the focus of the story more interior and psychological or exterior and action oriented?

The Thriller genre offers a clear-cut example of this distinction. Although action is an important part of their novels of Espionage, writers such as John le Carré and John Gardner (in his Herbie Kruger novels) take readers inside their characters; the sense of this interior, more cerebral focus stays with the readers. On the other hand, readers are more likely to recall the external action in novels by Robert Ludlum and Tom Clancy, even if their characters have introspective moments. We might designate the former novels character centered and the latter plot centered. Again, given the choice, readers can decide which type they are in the mood to read.

Frame

While pacing may often be the initial element readers use to select the books they are in the mood to read, frame—setting, atmosphere, background, and tone—may be the most pervasive. When we describe this element, we speak in terms of the tone of the book, which may be bleak, suspenseful, or upbeat. The feel of the book might be humorous, magical, or romantic. The atmosphere may seem foreboding, menacing, or more generally evocative. These adjectives reflect tone and alert the reader to the overall impression a book gives.

The easiest aspect of frame to identify may be setting, although by setting, here we do not mean geography, but something more. Anyone who reads Mysteries, for example, knows that there is more than one type of Mystery set in the South; unless a reader wants only Mysteries set in the South, no matter what, similar geographic settings do not necessarily mean that the books will have the same appeal. Look at an author like Sharyn McCrumb, who has two Mystery series with southern settings. One, featuring anthropologist Elizabeth MacPherson, is humorous, lighthearted, and somewhat romantic. Those books in the second, the Ballad series, are bleaker, thought provoking Mysteries that evoke the haunting music of the South's past. Setting as an element of appeal really means background, not geographic place.

Frame can also mean the type of detail provided in the book. For example, in today's popular "rich-and-famous" novels, such as those by Judith Krantz, it is not the location that is important to many readers, but the descriptive detail, the author's emphasis on elegant clothing, stylish decor, brand names, and gourmet dinners. If they do not find these descriptive elements in a "rich-and-famous" novel, some readers tell us that the book is not quite right, although they often may not understand why. This setting is a kind of atmosphere or tone which pervades the book, a feeling we get from reading it. To identify this atmosphere, we ask ourselves the following questions, summarized in Figure 3.4.

Figure 3.4
Questions to Consider to Identify Frame

---

1. Is the background detailed or minimal?
2. Does the frame affect the tone or atmosphere?
3. Is there a special background frame?

Is the background detailed or minimal?

Is there a lot of information or detail—historical detail, for example? Could the book take place elsewhere without altering its effect on readers? Does the action take place in any barnyard with a rustic feel, or is it set in a barnyard on the plains of Kansas just after the Civil War, as in Jeanne Williams's *No Roof but Heaven,* rich with explicit details of both the physical structures and the times?[9] Or are the novels simply stories dropped in to a specific time, as are Amanda Quick's Regency Romances? These books give a general impression of the period, but the dialogue and story are more important than setting. Does the author give many specific details or just a general impression?

Does the frame affect the tone or atmosphere?

A book's tone can make it suspenseful, light, romantic, comic, upbeat, or dark. Is the frame instrumental in creating that sense of mystery or foreboding? What impression, or feel, does the book give? Sometimes the frame generates the atmosphere and sets the tone more gracefully and effectively than any other technique, as in Horror and Romantic Suspense novels. The description of the atmosphere, or background, can determine how readers feel about a book, and some authors use this element more effectively than characters or action to set the stage. In Nora Roberts's *Carnal Innocence,* for example, the steamy southern heat and the enveloping atmosphere of decay are so dramatically evoked that they are almost tangible.[10] They effectively set the stage for violent murder.

Is there a special background frame?

Some authors create a special frame in which they set their novels, and this background interests some readers as much as the story itself. We have noticed this phenomenon particularly in conversations with readers of Mysteries, but this emphasis is true in other genres, too. For instance, in Ellis Peters's Brother Cadfael mysteries, set in twelfth-century Shrewsbury, England, the medieval frame is essential, and the details of medieval life and thought are as important to the appeal of each book as the mystery itself. In fact, many of the details Peters provides are not vital to the mystery; she uses them simply to create a special atmosphere. Many readers tell us how much they enjoy books with a distinctive ambience or sidelight—be it gardening, opera, theater, rare books, or antiques—and that they will enjoy almost any novel, regardless of subject, in which the author pays such meticulous attention to the background or frame.

Although we have considered each aspect of appeal separately in this chapter, a book's appeal is really based on a combination of the elements described above. One book may have the same kind of characters as another story, but the fact that the author gives it a lighter, less serious treatment can make the story appeal to a very different audience. Both Mary Stewart and T. H. White have written Arthurian fantasies, but White's madcap romp has a different appeal from Stewart's more serious, elegiac approach. The elements considered above are not the ultimate list of characteristics inherent in a book's appeal; rather, these are a beginning, a rudimentary listing of possible elements. The more that readers' advisors work at articulating appeal, the better we become at identifying the elements that constitute appeal and at asking the questions that quickly help us ascertain a book's appeal, as well as the kinds of books that appeal to a particular reader.

What we have described is a mindset, a way to focus the impressions we have gained from reading and gleaning information about books from patron comments, book jackets, and reviews. To think in terms of appeal simply means to use the thought processes that already take place when we consider books, to focus on their appeal rather than on subject or even genre. Instead of reading for plot details, we read with an eye to the range of a book's appeal.

Following this practice reaps several immediate benefits. First, we can readily identify the type of book that will not appeal to the readers we are assisting. For example, not all English Mysteries interest the same readers. An experienced readers' advisor would probably not suggest Agatha Christie's Miss Marple mysteries to readers who ask for more books like Sir Arthur Conan Doyle's Sherlock Holmes series. Readers' advisors quickly discover that, with respect to character, Christie's pleasant and elderly amateur, who has brought the art of detection to near perfection through seemingly innocuous gossip and idle curiosity, holds a different attraction than Conan Doyle's more reserved and intellectual sleuth. In fact, recognizing which books do not have the same appeal for readers is an easy and very useful result of employing this focus, and it makes us a true resource for patrons.

Another benefit of this mindset is that it allows us to talk intelligently about books we have not read or did not enjoy. We will never be able to read everything, and we do not personally like everything we read. However, neither fact should prevent us from sharing these books with readers who might enjoy them. We talk in more depth about both these eventualities in chapter 4, The Readers' Advisory Interview. It should be clear that focusing on appeal allows us to learn—without reading every book or enjoying everything we read—what makes a book popular with readers. The terminology of appeal then allows us to articulate this popularity and characterize more readily a book we either have not read or did not enjoy. Without either lowering our personal standards or denigrating a reader's taste, we can talk about nonstop action, characters we recognize from the first page, or a suspenseful atmosphere, and we can provide readers with enough clues to decide whether or not they want to read the book.

Using this technique also allows us to see the range of appeal in a book and helps us open our minds to the various ways a book might appeal to readers. Thinking in terms of appeal clarifies how the same book may appeal to two readers for different reasons. For example, one reader may relish the action and adventure of Nobel Prize winner Henryk Sienkiewicz's *With Fire and Sword*, while another may read it for the sense of time (the 1640s), the place (eastern Europe), and the political and social situations it describes.[11] Readers' advisors need to be open to the range of possible appeals in books.

Appeal also helps us cross genres, based on what readers tell us they enjoy, and introduce those readers to authors they probably would never have discovered on their own. Readers who like Mysteries that feature bumbling detectives as characters are likely responding to the humor, pacing, character development, relationships, and/or plot devices found in such books. The pleasure taken in bumbling detectives may lead to books featuring bumbling spies and hapless heroes of humorous Romances, not to mention humorously picaresque and eccentric characters caught in Fantasy worlds beyond their imagining. Readers' advisors can open up the library's collection to readers by communicating these appeal elements in discussions about books.

The strongest argument we have encountered for using appeal as the basis of readers' advisory work is that it allows us to remember and retrieve so much more about books we have read. Over the years, we have conducted nearly fifty readers' advisory workshops, all of which have included an exercise that demonstrates how appeal works in describing books. Participants are asked to think of a fiction book as we discuss appeal elements. After the presentation, they are divided into small groups and they describe their books, relying only on appeal, not on plot. The responses have been overwhelming. Librarians have found they can recall far more than they ever expected when they think about a book's appeal rather than its plot. The truly revealing part of this exercise, however, is that other members of the group, those who listened to the appeal-based descriptions, have found it far easier to decide whether or not they were in the mood to read the books. Patrons deserve the same opportunity.

Appeal frees us from reliance on plot summaries and from giving mini-booktalks by providing a framework on which we can attach all the information we know about an author or title—drawn from our personal reading of books, reviews, book jacket summaries, as well as what we have heard about a book or author from fans or colleagues. If we tie our readers' advisory interviews to mini-booktalks and to plot summaries, we may feel compelled to talk only about books we have read and, of those, only those whose plots we remember. Relying on appeal allows us to characterize comfortably an author or a genre as well as a specific title and make suggestions for a wider range of books than we could ever read ourselves.

Unfortunately, practice with more formal booktalking techniques has programmed us to think about plot first. Thus, changing from relating plot summaries to offering appeal-based descriptions takes practice. This is not to say that plot summaries are not valuable—we sometimes incorporate them into our appeal descriptions—but they are not as useful in isolation; they need to be enhanced with appeal. In chapter 7, Training, we discuss the importance of talking about books with staff so that this activity becomes an integral aspect of our routine. When we do this, we need to focus on appeal; we need to go back to describing books by the way they naturally affect us as readers. We practice—at first in incomplete sentences—describing books by their appeal, before we work on pulling the information into a cohesive whole, in the same way we used to practice summarizing plots. Knowing how useful this style is in working with readers, how it allows us to see what it is about a book that makes it popular, to characterize even works we do not personally enjoy, and to focus on what readers tell us as they describe what they enjoy reading, we see the importance of appeal in our readers' advisory service and work to make it routine.

In considering a book's appeal, readers' advisors should keep two final points in mind. First, although the above explanation of a book's appeal is closely tied to genre fiction, readers and readers' advisors know that the same connection to appeal exists among all types of books, even those not traditionally considered genre novels. All readers of fiction appreciate receiving suggestions of authors of the same caliber and appeal as those they enjoy, whatever the readers' tastes. Second, our readers' advisory skills allow us to suggest a wide range of potentially appealing authors to readers, and we need to be careful not to limit what we offer. We know from our own reading choices that we are not always looking for the same kind of book, and we need to be careful that we do not characterize readers too narrowly and think of a particular patron as enjoying only Thrillers, Mysteries, or any other type of novel or level of quality.

In many ways, readers' advisory seems an inexact, unstructured, undocumented discipline, but to the extent that there is a key, a formula, appeal seems to be it. Unraveling a book's appeal is best compared to working with, and ultimately solving, an intricate puzzle. Readers' advisors discover clues to appeal in the books themselves as well as in reference books, book jackets, and reviews. Then we compare our perceptions to those of other readers—staff and patrons—and synthesize all these elements into an understanding of a book's appeal. Finally, we develop a vocabulary that builds on the way we naturally think about books and allows us to share them more easily.

Understanding the appeal of books and authors, and putting the information we glean from reading and hearing about books in a framework structured around appeal elements, allows us to offer a range of titles to readers. Since we are simply building on a natural tendency, we relate more easily to the way readers choose books and are not deterred by the feeling that there is only one perfect book that will satisfy readers each time they come to the library. Thinking in terms of appeal allows us to respond to patron tastes with a range of titles that might interest them.

In our experience, the more we work with appeal and the more we allow appeal—the way we naturally reflect on books—to structure our readers' advisory interviews, the more successful and satisfying these interactions become. Thinking in terms of appeal allows us to see what an author does best—character, story, or perhaps atmosphere. We can identify the feel of the book, the impressions readers take away. We can talk about books we have not read or did not like because we can readily gain information about appeal without actually reading every book we talk about. In the next chapter, we explore ways in which we use appeal and reference sources in working directly with readers.

Notes

1. Anna Quindlen, *One True Thing* (New York: Random, 1994).
2. *NoveList* CD-ROM, Carl Corporation, Denver, Colo., 1994.
3. Thomas Harris, *The Silence of the Lambs* (New York: St. Martin's, 1988).
4. Peter Høeg, *Smilla's Sense of Snow* (New York: Farrar, 1993); Martin Cruz Smith, *Gorky Park* (New York: Random, 1981).
5. Elizabeth Adler, *The Rich Shall Inherit* (New York: Delacorte, 1989).
6. Robert Graves, *I, Claudius* (New York: Random, 1961).
7. Michael Shaara, *The Killer Angels* (New York: McKay, 1974).
8. Jane Smiley, *A Thousand Acres* (New York: Knopf, 1991).
9. Jeanne Williams, *No Roof but Heaven* (New York: St. Martin's, 1990).
10. Nora Roberts, *Carnal Innocence* (New York: Bantam, 1991).
11. Henryk Sienkiewicz, *With Fire and Sword*, W. S. Kuniczak, trans. (New York: Hippocrene, 1991).

4 The Readers' Advisory Interview

Ⅰn this chapter, we consider one of the basics of readers' advisory service: the readers' advisory interview. We describe the interview and then examine the preparation and skills needed to become an adept readers' advisor. We believe that to become proficient in conducting readers' advisory interviews, librarians must direct the way we think about books and adopt a method of thinking that becomes second nature and that can then be applied both to books we read and to those we read about. Along with formalizing a way of thinking about books comes the necessity of learning to talk about books, of putting mental observations and impressions about books into words. We provide suggestions for doing this as well. We discuss how the interview works, ranging from ways to open a conversation with readers to possible ways to respond to reader queries. Finally, we describe some special situations, based on occurrences from our experience as readers' advisors. Experienced readers' advisors will recognize problems they have encountered, while new readers' advisors will see the range of situations they might eventually face and have a chance to think about how they might deal with them.

A Definition

The readers' advisory interview, on its most elementary level, is a conversation between the advisor and the reader about books. A readers' advisor will certainly use all the same communication skills involved in reference interviewing to get readers to describe their reading tastes and what they are in the mood to read at the time. Yet, unlike a reference interview, the readers' advisory interview is not primarily a question-and-answer exchange; it is a conversation, with readers telling the readers' advisor about books and their tastes in fiction, and the readers' advisor listening and suggesting possible titles. The measure of success for the readers' advisory interview is not whether the reader takes and reads the books the readers' advisor offers. Rather, the exchange is a success when readers perceive, based on the service they receive, that the library is a place where they can talk about books and obtain suggestions and resources to meet their reading needs. A successful readers' advisory interview is not, nor should it be, a one-time encounter. The advisor encourages readers to return and give their reactions to the books suggested, thus establishing an ongoing dialogue between readers and the readers' advisory staff.

Since the readers' advisory interview usually occurs in an open area, it is rarely a two-person encounter. Fortunately, readers are notorious eavesdroppers when they hear books being discussed. Other patrons often chime in with their impressions and suggestions of possible book titles. The readers' advisor may describe several books to one patron only to have them disappear from the shelves as a soon as the readers' advisor and the patron turn their backs. Or a patron may say, "Last time I was in, you were telling another woman about a novel that took place during the Irish Potato Famine. It sounded so good that I'd like to read it." The trick, then, is to remember which book was being discussed.

Before we proceed further, we need to address two issues: the distinction between *suggesting* and *recommending* books and the question of quality, specifically the use of the phrase "well written." Although the distinction between *suggest* and *recommend* may seem a trivial question of semantics, our terminology preference is important. We do far better readers' advisory when we stop using these words interchangeably. When we talk with friends, we likely *recommend* titles we want them to read, based on our personal knowledge of their interests or perhaps because we want someone else to read and then discuss a title with us. When we work with readers in a library, we talk with them about what they might enjoy reading. We then *suggest* a range of books that might appeal to them, based on what they have said about their reading tastes, interests, and mood.

When we make this distinction, when we *suggest* rather than *recommend*, we change the focus of our readers' advisory and of our patron interactions. It is far less threatening to talk with a reader and suggest a range of books than to take the responsibility for recommending something we think is appropriate. Patrons are also more comfortable returning with comments, especially negative comments, about books we have suggested than about those that come recommended. We all know how difficult it is to tell someone that we really did not like the book they insisted we would love. Suggestions establish a friendly, professional link between librarian and reader. They allow readers to choose whether to read a book or not, as well as freedom to like a book or not.

The manner in which we describe "quality" fiction is another, more difficult, issue. At our library we try to avoid the phrase "well written." Our main objection is that the phrase means almost nothing to the reader who hears it. We may have a group of authors or titles to which we apply this term, but all readers have their own favorites, books they consider well written. We have all heard readers apply "well written" to the gamut of fiction, no matter how critics review the writing style, from award-winners to paperback originals. When readers connect with a book, when it satisfies them, they view it as well written. For example, Duncan Smith suggests that readers who enjoy fast-paced, action-oriented novels may not consider a book such as Ishiguro's *Remains of the Day,* winner of Great Britain's prestigious Booker Prize, well written because it does not meet their personal standards for a well-written, satisfying book.[1] In Ishiguro's novel, the pacing is very slow, as the author takes his time revealing character and story line, and readers who prefer more action may not be satisfied. At the Downers Grove Public Library, we have found it far more useful and informative to talk about the way an author uses language or an unusual or distinctive style if such comments seem relevant. We might also describe a book as an "award-winner" or "critically acclaimed" if we believe a reader would relate to this appeal. In the readers' advisory interview, "well written" has become an empty catchall phrase; unfortunately, relying on it to describe a "quality" title is a hard habit to break, as we know from experience.

The job of the readers' advisor is to suggest books, based on information received from readers about their reading tastes and moods. This is not to say that the question of quality—the way a book is written—is not a considered part of the discussion. By asking the librarian for suggestions, the patron assumes the librarian is aware of a book's quality and will not offer books of dramatically lesser quality than those the patron usually reads. Nor is there the presumption that only the "best" will be suggested, for not everyone who likes Romances, for example, will be pleased with Jane Austen. Some readers may enjoy Austen or a classic Historical Romance writer such as Georgette Heyer. Fans of newer popular Historical Romance authors, such as Marion Chesney or Patricia Veryan, may be interested in Austen or Heyer, but they may also appreciate other critically acclaimed and award-winning authors such as Jo Beverly or Amanda Quick. As a professional, the readers' advisory librarian is expected to be aware of both the appeal of a book and its general quality. Even when readers express a desire for something of lesser quality than they usually read, something "light" or an "easy read," it is important to verify first the type of book and then the level of quality the reader has in mind and to be aware that there are levels and variations at both ends of this quality spectrum.

To repeat, then, a readers' advisory interview is a conversation between the advisor and the reader about books. The goal is to establish the idea of this service in the minds of readers so they know that readers' advisory is a legitimate library activity. Using many of the same communication skills that reference interviewers use, the readers' advisor tries to get a picture of the type of books the reader enjoys, makes some suggestions—perhaps using or referring the patron to special reference resources—and invites the reader to return. In the next section we will discuss the preparation and skills that are needed to conduct successful interviews.

Preparing for the Interview

Thinking about Books

If you are a reader, you know that sharing a good book is one of the joys of life. One of the pleasures of doing readers' advisory is just that—sharing books with people. We have all had the experience of reading a book and thinking immediately of a friend who would also enjoy reading it. While sharing books with friends is usually based on a history of mutual experiences and interests, approaching an anonymous or relatively unknown library patron and suggesting a book is quite another matter. Yet such "informal" encounters comprise almost all the book suggestions readers' advisors make in a library. It is important to understand how to share books with readers so that, with practice, a readers' advisor can talk with almost anyone about books and reading.

Preparation for the readers' advisory interview begins long before the dialogue with a patron takes place. The real key to successful readers' advisory is in learning how to *think* about books, a three-phase process. First, readers' advisors begin with the book's appeal, what makes the book a "good read." Second, advisors group the book with other titles and authors that have similar appeal. Third, readers' advisors consider how authors and titles fit within a genre.

To some people this whole thought process comes naturally. Not only can they remember almost every book they have ever read, but they can talk about books in a way that makes us want to read them immediately. Fortunately, readers' advisory is an art that involves techniques that those of us who lack this talent naturally can learn, practice, and master. These techniques are relatively easy to learn. In fact, if you are a reader, you probably already use them unconsciously.

The first technique—reading a book with an eye to its appeal—goes against many of our English teachers' instructions to read critically to identify themes, symbols, etc. Reading to do readers' advisory in preparation for suggesting books to other readers grows naturally from our own enjoyment of books. In talking with a friend, for instance, we describe our reactions to a book. As a readers' advisor, we simply need to expand this viewpoint, to ask, What is it about the book that would appeal to another reader?

When reading, readers' advisors watch for a book's best feature: characterization, frame, pacing, or story line. Sometimes more than one element stands out, but often a single feature strikes us. For example, in a particular Thriller, the key to the book's appeal may be the strong, sympathetic hero. In another book, it may be the exotic setting or the fascinating historical detail. In still another book, the appeal may be witty dialogue or insight into problems. In describing Patricia Cornwell's Mysteries, which feature a medical examiner, it is easy to identify the wealth of medical detail they contain, whether we have read Cornwell's books or only heard about them. With Clive Cussler, we might focus on the adventure element and the range of background material he brings to his books. The key is to read with the goal of discovering the appeal, identifying it, and describing—even if only mentally—what seems to be the book's best feature or features. We found this exercise to be invaluable when we began to talk about books with other readers, because focusing on the appeal made talking about books easier and more natural. We also note any of the book's unusual details: The book may provide interesting insights about antiques and the antique business, or the etchings that illustrate the book may have been done by the author. These elements are sometimes a wonderful draw for patrons, so they are worth noting.

While readers' advisors are looking for a book's best features, they should also be alert to characteristics that might limit its appeal. For example, might the amount of explicit sex or violence offend some readers? Does the author employ an unconventional style, such as stream of consciousness, which may annoy some readers? Does the book advocate a particular political or social position? Does it address social or moral issues that some readers might find offensive? None of these characteristics should necessarily keep a readers' advisor from suggesting a particular book, however. While certain elements may bother some readers, they may be the very features that attract others. Readers' advisors simply need to be aware of the presence of these elements. In the next section, Talking about Books, and later in Special Situations, we discuss more fully how to handle those aspects which may limit a book's appeal to certain readers.

After we started identifying a book's appeal to readers, we found ourselves moving on to the second phase: grouping books with other authors and titles that have similar appeal. Basically, when we finish a book, we simply ask ourselves what other books are like it, what other books would appeal to the reader who enjoyed this one. We think about the particular kinds of characters, story line, pacing, point of view—all of the elements that affect a book's appeal. That two books feature amateur detectives does not necessarily mean they would both appeal to the same reader, unless other elements work together to give the books the same feel. For example, the admirers of Lawrence Block's burglar/detective/rare books dealer Bernie Rhodenbarr would not automatically consider Diane Mott Davidson's Goldie Bear, caterer cum sleuth, to be of the same ilk.

It is not always possible to come up with similar books and authors, even after having practiced this technique for years. However, the mental exercise of trying to think of other books with the same appeal strengthens our ability to group similar authors and titles. We have found that, with practice, it is even possible—and extremely useful—to apply this comparative questioning technique to books for which we have read only the reviews or that we have heard discussed by friends and patrons. Readers' advisors become attuned to clues that signal similar appeal for readers and are thus able to link books with greater ease.

The third phase in learning how to think about books—considering how a book fits within a genre—continues the practice of grouping similar authors and titles. When working with a genre, librarians often find it useful to look for dissimilar authors. For example, if we read a Fantasy by Stephen Donaldson and realize that it is not like those by Robert Lynn Asprin, we have made an important and useful distinction within the Fantasy genre. It is often easier, in fact, to identify like authors after eliminating those that are dissimilar. The ability to recognize why authors and titles are similar or dissimilar expands our understanding of the genre. We readers' advisors find ourselves creating a framework that allows us to characterize genres and to place authors within those genres.

The ability to group authors and titles also helps a readers' advisor link books in which the similarities may not be immediately obvious. For example, a reader of Robert Ludlum's Espionage Thrillers may like not only Dick Francis's Mysteries but also Westerns by Louis L'Amour. All these works feature strong heroes and action-filled plots, although the settings differ. Having successfully identified a book's appeal, readers' advisors will find that they can expand readers' horizons beyond such elements as time or setting, which would seem to separate books. By the same token, Romance readers who enjoy the sophisticated world of the upper class as portrayed in some Contemporary Romances may also enjoy Regency Romances, even though they are set almost two hundred years earlier. Both provide a glimpse of the fashionable world of the period—clothes, language, important personages—in addition to the romance.

Even after readers' advisors have mastered this method of thinking about books—of reading for the book's appeal, grouping similar authors and titles, and linking books within a genre—one essential component still remains: *Readers' advisors need a way to remember what they have read.* We all know the frustration of not having enough time to read everything we would like to read (not to mention everything library patrons believe we have read or ought to have read). However, it is just as disconcerting not to remember the title of a wonderful book that would be just right to suggest to a particular reader or to add to a display. There are undoubtedly many solutions to this problem, and it is important to find one that suits each advisor. We like ours for its simplicity. We each keep a notebook with a list of the authors and titles we have read, drawing a line between months. Adding a code letter next to each work can help to further differentiate book by genre.

How could any device this simple help us remember the dozens of books we read each year? You would be surprised. Because the list is chronological and divided by month, it is possible to place a book in time among other books read, and that information alone often jogs our memory of the book. When we look at a title on our list, checking the dates and the titles that appear before and after it will often bring the book vividly to mind. We can recall much of the plot, characters, and feel of the book. This is not to say that this method gives us instant recall of every book we have read, but it does give us a better chance to remember the book. Nevertheless, keeping a list of what we have read is not enough. We must also review the list frequently. This practice refreshes our memory and even allows us to make connections between books that we might otherwise have missed. Looking back over the list, we often realize that the book we just read is similar to something we read several years earlier. In chapter 5, we discuss a more formal method of recording what we and others have read: a system of annotation cards.

To be a readers' advisor, we need to learn how to think about books. Once we have mastered the techniques of identifying a book's appeal and started keeping track of what we read, we will see the rewards in our expanding knowledge of books and how we relate to readers. Having thought through and used these techniques, readers' advisors develop a way of looking at books that allows us to evoke useful responses from patrons and to help readers define their reading interests.

Talking about Books

As readers' advisors master the art of thinking about books, we also need to practice talking about books. As we pointed out above, the more that readers' advisors practice identifying the appeal of the books we read, the easier it becomes to recognize that appeal. In the same way, the more that advisors describe books by their appeal, the more skilled we become. Verbalizing our opinions provides the acid test for some of our pet theories about books. Talking about a book's appeal with others—friends, staff, and patrons—takes readers' advisors out of the vacuum of simply reading and thinking about books. It gives us an opportunity to test our opinions about a book's appeal and to hone our interviewing skills.

We readers' advisors find out quickly which approaches work and learn to refine our technique accordingly. It is primarily through talking with others about books that readers' advisors discover which questions work in a readers' advisory interview—i.e., which questions elicit responses from readers and which do not.

It is easiest to practice talking about books informally. While we listen to someone describe a book, we attempt to understand its appeal and group it with books we know. We find ourselves asking mentally, Who else writes that kind of book? or What other book is it like? These are the same questions we ask ourselves when we finish reading a book. If a friend liked one book and not another we thought was similar, we ask why. For example, we suggested Stephen Coonts's Military Adventures to a reader of W.E.B. Griffin. The reader came back to say these books were not exactly what he had in mind. He explained that Coonts was too technical for his taste, and what he enjoyed about Griffin were the stories. Another Storyteller with military themes, such as Joe Weber, was a better match. Framing questions to elicit this information will be discussed later.

Informal encounters not only allow readers' advisors to test our opinions about books and authors; they can also be excellent sources of information about good reading—books to pass on to other readers. We encourage friends, colleagues, and patrons to tell us about books they have enjoyed. After all, at its best readers' advisory is a two-way street, involving both the giving and taking of suggestions. In a library where this atmosphere of sharing books exists, readers' advisors will find more and more patrons talking about books with each other and even suggesting titles they have enjoyed to total strangers. We have been amazed at the amount of book sharing that goes on. However, readers' advisors need to be prepared for the consequences of this situation. We often find ourselves in a hopeless state of having more books suggested to us than we will ever be able to read.

In addition, a library staff that thinks and talks about books is a great asset. In the best of all possible worlds (and libraries), talking about books, sharing what we read, is not limited to a single department. Readers' advisory work flourishes in an atmosphere in which it is not unusual to talk about books; and the more that books are discussed throughout the library, the more the people actually doing readers' advisory will benefit. When discussing books becomes an accepted and welcome part of staff interactions among librarians themselves and with patrons, the library's visibility as a resource for readers grows.

These informal discussions with friends, patrons, and colleagues are extremely useful for validating readers' advisors' perceptions about what they read, for gleaning additional reading suggestions, and for creating an atmosphere in which books are discussed. However, they are not a substitute for scheduled discussions among the readers' advisory staff. There are many ways to handle such discussions. In *The Fair Garden and the Swarm of Beasts*, Margaret A. Edwards describes the process whereby she trained her new young adult assistants, prescribing a list of three hundred books for them to read and discuss with her![2] Our own approach, which includes a much more limited directed reading plan that is described in chapter 5, is less structured. The department meets monthly, and we always begin these meetings by talking about what each of us is currently reading. From this experience, we refine our ability to describe a book by its appeal, and we learn from our own attempts as well as from listening to others. We pick up additional information about books and related authors and titles from other experienced readers' advisors, and we rather effortlessly expand our familiarity with books that we can later share with patrons. We also have a chance to bring up and discuss problems, such as books for which similar authors and titles are not immediately obvious.

No matter what our situation, it is important to set up opportunities to talk about books with others who do readers' advisory directly or who understand how readers' advisors think and talk about books, whether in our own libraries or outside. There is simply no substitute for the opportunity to practice talking about books among colleagues in a setting away from patrons.

For further inspiration and examples of the joy of talking about books, have a look at Christopher Morley's *Parnassus on Wheels* and Helene Hanff's *84, Charing Cross Road*.[3] In fact, we have made them required reading for our staff, not because these works follow our suggested techniques, but because they are wonderful examples of people who treasure books and can talk about them in a way that makes you want to do so, too.

Setting the Stage

When we begin our shift at busy service desks, we can expect to be bombarded with a variety of requests from patrons, ranging from business statistics to information on obscure medical disorders and much more. One of the biggest obstacles readers' advisors face is making the almost instantaneous shift from providing specific factual information using a range of highly technical sources to serving the patron who wants a good book to read or several books for vacation reading, requests for which there may be no sources to consult. Making this kind of mental leap is no easy task. Strategies to deal with this situation are vital for all readers' advisors, from the newest to the most experienced.

We have found that the following warm-up exercises help prepare us for the rigors of making these dramatic shifts in focus and technique. If we have practiced thinking and talking about books, we have already accomplished a great deal of this preparation. The following techniques, when part of our desk routine, require only two to three minutes early in our shift and are invaluable in helping us mentally set the stage for encounters with readers.

First, whenever we work at the service desk, we check the bookshelves in the area in which most fiction readers browse. Some libraries separate newer books from the rest of the collection, and it is often the newer books that first attract patrons. Others have special display areas where patrons congregate. Whatever the arrangement, when readers' advisors are at the public service desk, we need to know what is on these shelves because these are the books we can most easily draw on to do readers' advisory. It is impossible to browse the entire fiction collection, but spending a few minutes previewing a manageable area not only gives us an idea of what is available that day but also starts us thinking about books. We look for titles in the genres or subgenres that our patrons request most often—Serial Murders, Legal Thrillers, Romances, or whatever else is being asked for at the library—and we start thinking about how we would describe the titles to patrons. It is especially useful for us to identify titles in popular genres with which we are less familiar; doing so increases our familiarity with the genre and prepares us for patrons' requests. We also keep in mind some possible title suggestions for our regulars—those patrons who come in routinely; nothing pleases them more than a good book they have somehow missed. If we have time, we glance at a few book jacket summaries as well, in order to learn about unfamiliar titles. This is a good time to check our displays and add titles. We try to have several book displays highlighting subjects or types of fiction, in addition to our permanent Good Books You May Have Missed display. (These are discussed in more detail in chapter 6.) In the latter display, which features older and sometimes overlooked titles in our collection, we try to ensure that we have a range of genres represented. Filling the displays gets us into the stacks, handling books and thinking how we might share them with readers.

Second, we check what is currently on the best-sellers list. We post the *New York Times* best-sellers list from the weekly *New York Times Book Review* near our recent fiction and keep another copy at our desk. This list is especially useful because the short synopsis that accompanies each title is often just enough to jog our memory of what a particular book is about.

We also check to see if copies of best-sellers are on the shelf. Unless your library is far better stocked than ours, you will know that such a possibility is unlikely. The answer to this dilemma is to consider what other authors might appeal to the reader seeking a specific best-seller. For example, when Stephen King appears on the best-sellers list, we supply a lot of other Horror fiction, such as that written by Dean R. Koontz and Dan Simmons, to readers who are waiting their turn for King's new book. The same principle applies to any other best-selling authors. It is important for us to know which authors we may be asked for so that we can be prepared to suggest other possibilities when a patron requests authors and titles that are too popular to be available on the shelves.

The final warm-up suggestion involves keeping a log or notes of readers' advisory requests. In the beginning we kept such a log, which listed requests followed by the books suggested by the staff, and we checked it whenever we came on the desk. This started us thinking generally about readers' advisory requests and alerted us to currently requested authors and topics so that we could be prepared for similar questions. We no longer routinely keep a log, but we do have a notebook in which we keep track of questions we are working on so staff at the readers' advisory desk can continue these searches. Reviewing this notebook allows us to see trends in requests and book suggestions. Keeping and referring to these questions gives us a chance to think about how we would handle them if asked.

The Readers' Advisory Interview

Unlike patrons with reference questions, who generally approach us to ask for assistance, most readers are reluctant to ask librarians for reading suggestions. Only when readers have been helped and are made comfortable coming to the desk do we find substantial numbers of readers asking us directly for assistance.

More often, readers come to the desk to ask about a specific author, or sometimes a genre. They may have been reading Mary Higgins Clark and are looking for more of her titles. Or they want the new Danielle Steel novel that just came out today. In the cases of these popular authors, once we have answered the immediate question, finding another title by Clark or taking a reserve for the Steel novel, we might ask, Do you also read Joy Fielding? for the Clark fan, or Have you discovered Katherine Stone? for the Steel reader. These are useful ways to start a readers' advisory conversation. These questions show readers that we are knowledgeable, that we can make suggestions, and that talking about books—and particularly about similar authors—is accepted behavior, the kind of request they should be comfortable making at our desk.

What about the reader who asks us for a best-seller? If your library is like ours, the book is unlikely to be available for immediate checkout. In our experience, however, the majority of the people who come to the library are looking for a good, satisfying read, and the John Sandford novel of Suspense they just read about in the paper is their own suggestion as a possibility to fill this need. Another author, such as David Wiltse for the Sandford reader, may be a very satisfying suggestion to tide them over while they are awaiting their turn for the Sandford. By the way, we should also be open to the possibility that readers may not even really want the kind of fiction they ask for when identifying an author on the best-sellers list. Sandford may simply be a name someone gave them, and in talking further, we may find something else much more satisfying.

The final way readers' advisory interviews begin is when we approach browsers in the book stacks. Although some readers approach readers' advisors for suggestions, in most cases readers' advisors need to make the initial contact. Our offer of assistance is designed to let patrons know that we are there to suggest books. In our experience, questions such as, Is there a special book you are looking for? or May I suggest something to read? are more likely to elicit a response than the question, Can I help you? With the latter, readers are unlikely to feel that suggesting titles and discussing their reading tastes is what we have in mind. When we talk with readers, we try to reinforce the idea that suggesting books is a service we routinely provide.

Most patrons do not expect to find a readers' advisory service in the library. In fact, many patrons would not consider asking for reading suggestions to be a valid request. Recent research suggests that among the top four reasons fiction readers do not ask for assistance is that "a question about fiction (which is unimportant) would be perceived as being frivolous and waste staff time."[4] They would not hesitate to ask questions such as, Do you have information on how to fix a broken washing machine? or, When was the Chicago Fire? But, curiously, asking for a good Espionage novel does not occur to them as being a permissible question. Readers' advisors need to validate the fact that talking about books is a legitimate activity for both the librarian and the reader.

We believe that librarians must be aggressive in offering this service to patrons. For the most part, readers' advisory interviews do not just happen. Readers' advisors cannot wait for the patron to ask about a book; instead, we must seek out patrons. Our staff tries to speak to every patron who comes into the fiction area. Some additional approaches we use include: Would you like some suggestions, or are you comfortable browsing? Are you finding what you are looking for, or could I suggest something for you? and simply, May I suggest something for you to read? We have found that these are all effective ways to alert patrons to the readers' advisory service the department provides. Patrons looking puzzled or leaving the area without a book are often responsive to an offer of assistance.

Whenever we receive repeated requests for a certain kind of book, we take advantage of this fact and incorporate it into our approach. For instance, the comment, Looking for something light for the summer? makes a good beginning on hot July days. We always make sure we have some titles in mind for the patron who readily agrees. If patrons say no, they often feel the need to explain: "No, I'm looking for something more like Stephen King. Do you know anyone like him?" Then we have a clue as to what to offer.

Clearly, readers' advisory, like any other public service work in a library, cannot be done solely from behind a desk; librarians need to be in the stacks with the books and the readers. We use every opportunity to reinforce with our patrons the idea that the role of the readers' advisory staff is to suggest books to readers, that we know popular fiction, and that readers should feel free to talk with us about their reading interests. We recognize that some patrons prefer to browse on their own; and while we respect their privacy, we also want to be sure that they know the service is available. They cannot use a service they do not know exists. We work to be helpful without being intrusive. Readers may not talk with us the first time, but they often feel safe approaching us when they return to the library. With just a few words we have set the stage for future encounters, which often develop into long-term relationships between readers' advisory staff and readers.

Once we have the reader's attention, we need information in order to make suggestions. Traditional questions such as, What do you like to read? usually do not elicit helpful information because patrons can rarely come up with a useful answer on the spur of the moment, and then they feel foolish. We have found a better approach is to ask, Tell me about a book you really enjoyed. Or, Is there an author you consistently read? Even asking, Have you read anything lately that you disliked? can start a useful exchange. Readers often find it easier to describe a book they did not enjoy, giving us valuable information that we can use in suggesting more appropriate titles and authors. Readers are surprisingly forthcoming in describing both what they enjoy and what they do not. A patron might say, "The last book I read was too slow; nothing ever happened," or "I just didn't like the characters." Both responses provide clues that, with some rephrasing, can help patrons recognize what they *do* like. For example, we may reply: "What about a book with a lot of action. Maybe a Thriller or an Adventure story?"

If this approach still does not provide enough information, we describe the special characteristics of books: "Do you like a book with a fast-moving plot or one with strong characters?" Offering the reader a choice allows the readers' advisor to narrow the range of possible suggestions. If the reader responds to the fast-moving plot, the next question might be, Have you read any Mysteries or Thrillers? as both types of books may have fast-moving plots; or at this point we might describe the features of a popular Crime Storyteller such as Stuart Woods.

It is also important to try to discover characteristics of books that *do not* appeal to particular patrons. After all, the goal of readers' advisory is to give the patrons what they want and are comfortable reading. For example, we note preferences as to time period and setting. We all know patrons who would prefer not to read books that have frank language or explicit sex. A tactful way to elicit this information is to ask if there are books the patron may not have enjoyed. If we are not sure exactly what to suggest, we offer a range of books. If a reader says she enjoys Romances, for example, but is not more specific, we might show her a Contemporary Romance, one of the more romantic Gentle Reads, and a Sensual Historical Romance. Patrons' responses give us clues to their preferences.

As readers tell us what they enjoy or what they dislike, we listen for the appeal elements and how patrons express them. Fans of John Grisham's Legal Thrillers may enjoy another writer in the same genre, perhaps someone like Steve Martini, but they may also simply be looking for another fast-paced, engrossing book. Or perhaps they would like one that features a similar type of character:

the innocent who discovers treachery in those he thought to trust, and who then fights to save his life and expose the danger. For this reader, Philip Shelby's *Days of Drums*, featuring a secret service agent caught up in a plot to kill the president, may fill the bill.[5] From having considered the range of ways a book might appeal, we now fall back on that knowledge and listen for the clues patrons give us about the types of books they are looking for or do not enjoy. Having mastered the idea of appeal, we can respond appropriately to patrons' requests for similar titles.

If possible, we like to suggest at least three titles, giving the patron an overview of each one and describing each generally in terms of appeal. Here is where we put into play all the book-describing skills we have been practicing. For example, we will talk about what is best in the book, special features that might appeal to readers, how the book fits into the genre, or what other readers have said about it. We may not want to refer to all these factors every time, but these are some of the elements we draw on in talking about books. It is important to recognize that we do not necessarily need to know the plot of every title we describe; we talk instead in terms of appeal, highlighting aspects patrons have said they enjoy. Describing several possible titles reinforces the concept that readers' advisors suggest rather than recommend, thus allowing the reader to make the final selection. We are not providing the one and only "perfect book" for the reader. Since readers typically have a wide range of tastes, there are usually several possible books they would find satisfying. We suggest several so they can make choices, in the library and at home, about what they are in the mood to read.

We should also say that readers' advisory inquiries, like many reference questions, do not necessarily require immediate responses. Some patrons are perfectly happy to have us take notes about the kind of book or author they are interested in and then call them later with suggestions. This gives us an opportunity to discuss queries with fellow staff members and to follow leads in reference materials at our leisure. We frequently leave difficult-to-answer patron requests in the notebook at our desk and solicit suggestions from other staff members. A patron who is looking for something specific usually does not mind the wait and, what is more, appreciates the interest and personal attention. In addition, we have validated the importance of their question.

Putting books in patrons' hands is not the end of the readers' advisory interview; it is equally important to close with an invitation for the reader to return. Since more than one person does readers' advisory in our library, it is especially important to establish that whoever is working at the readers' advisory desk can provide this service, not just the person the patron is talking to. We encourage patrons to check back and tell the readers' advisor on duty what they enjoyed and, even more important, what they did not care for, as that also provides useful information. When readers' advisors assure readers that they are interested not only in what readers enjoyed but also in the books that were not quite right, they are reinforcing the idea that the readers' opinions are valued and that there are many more titles that might appeal to them. Advising patrons is a process in which the readers' advisors work not only with what they know about literature but also with what the reader brings to the exchange.

Although we describe the readers' advisory interview as a conversation about books, it does have a structure that closely parallels one many of us have learned in order to conduct better reference interviews. In the early 1980s, unobtrusive testing in Maryland public libraries revealed that the correct answer to reference questions was provided only about fifty-five percent of the time. To improve this situation, a model for the reference interview was developed and used successfully in Maryland and across the country.

The interview process was broken down into four stages.[6] The first stage, Setting the Tone, emphasizes approachability. Librarians smile, make eye contact, and greet patrons. In stage two, Getting the Facts, the process stresses showing interest in the patron and the question, paraphrasing and clarifying the patron request, asking open-ended questions to solicit further information, and negotiating the inquiry by thoroughly consulting sources. Giving Information constitutes stage three. Here, all the earlier techniques come into play, as does citing sources. Finally, stage four requires a follow-up query: "Does this completely answer your question?"

It takes little effort to apply these steps to the readers' advisory interview. Approachability—welcoming body language and acknowledging the patron—sets the stage; readers need to be made comfortable asking librarians for assistance, especially with questions about reading suggestions, which so many readers have been taught to see as less important than "real" reference questions.

As in a reference interview, we need to get the facts in stage two, although fiction readers often have more nebulous questions than do patrons seeking specific information. When readers describe the kinds of books they enjoy, we follow up by paraphrasing their response. "It sounds as if what you enjoy about Tom Clancy's

Thrillers is all the technical detail and action, as well as the community of men, and the fact that the hero solves the problem through ingenuity." The next question follows automatically: "Are you in the mood for something like that, or would you rather have something different today?" Whether our searches lead us to the fiction shelves, to catalogs of our collection, to book or electronic resources, to displays, and/or to book lists, we involve the readers in the search to validate the importance of their questions.

As we provide information, we highlight the appeal elements of the books, emphasizing those elements in which the reader has already expressed an interest. If readers do not provide specific information, we ask probing questions: "Do you like a lot of action in your books, or do you prefer to know the characters very well?" As we said earlier, we offer a range of titles and encourage readers to take several. We can also use appeal to introduce readers to authors or genres they may not be familiar with. If a reader enjoys Tom Clancy but talks also about a preference for strong, interesting characters, we might also suggest an author such as John Gardner. We might point out that Gardner's Herbie Kruger books have a series character like Clancy's, but that the books have less technical detail and more cerebral twists and turns of plot, as well as more emphasis on characterization. We provide readers with information about authors and titles and allow them to make their own choices. We have not said this book is just like what they read or guaranteed that they will enjoy it. We offer a range of books and give the readers the kind of information they need to make a decision.

Finally, just as in the reference interview model, we ask a follow up question at the end of the interview. In this case, it is not whether we have completely answered the question. As we have already pointed out, in readers' advisory work there is almost never one right answer. Rather, readers' advisors follow up by encouraging readers to come back and tell whoever is on the desk whether they liked the books or not. We encourage them to return for further suggestions, stressing that there are so many books that, whether they like these titles or not, there are always others they might find satisfying.

Even though we emphasize the process of suggesting and describing individual books to readers, the goal is not primarily to get readers to take home the particular book we suggest. Certainly nothing is so satisfying as to have patrons seek us out and tell us how much they enjoyed the book we previously suggested to them. As rewarding as that can be, however, readers' advisory would be very frustrating and limiting if that response were all we expected from the exchange. Patrons do not always take the books we think they will like, and they foolishly dislike things we just know are "perfect" for them. The true measure of the success of the service is not the number of books taken out but the frequency and quality of readers' advisory exchanges.

In summary, there are two important points to remember about the readers' advisory interview. First, we are suggesting, not recommending, a range of books in which a reader might be interested. We are not looking for one perfect book; rather, we offer possibilities. Second, readers usually are not looking for books on a particular subject; they are looking for books with a certain feel, and we do better when we share books in these terms. Thus, while it is helpful to be able to identify books by subject, we, as readers, all know there can be real differences between them. In Historical Mysteries, for example, a comparison of Peter Lovesey's humorous Mysteries, which feature Bertie, the Prince of Wales, and Anne Perry's much bleaker Inspector Monk stories, demonstrates that not all historical mysteries are the same.

Acknowledging this, we need to rethink how we describe books to readers. Mini-booktalks are not necessarily the answer. The responsibility of giving a mini-booktalk for every book we suggest puts us under a lot of pressure. For one thing, it implies we know and can describe the plot of every book. It even suggests that we have read all the books we talk about with readers and remember them well enough to describe them and, thus, that to do our best readers' advisory, we should limit ourselves to books we know and remember. Such thinking puts us all in a real bind. However, if, in describing books to readers, we focus on appeal elements, we do better. Not only can we remember more about books we have read or read about if we think about them in terms of appeal, we can also talk invitingly about books that we have not read and know much less about.

This approach takes practice and changing our focus as we read and read about books, but it is really no harder than giving the mini-booktalks we now do. We start by considering what an author does best. All our practice thinking and talking about books helps to prepare us for this approach, which capitalizes on appeal—the way we naturally think about books—and enables us to present the kind of information to readers that allows them to choose for themselves what to read.

Special Situations

The following examples, which portray situations readers' advisors are sure to encounter, will clarify the nature of the readers' advisory interview. The examples are based on questions we have been asked, and the responses reflect what has worked for us; however, they are not necessarily the only, or even the best, ways to handle each case. Other readers' advisors will undoubtedly work out their own strategies.

How do we talk about a book or genre we have not read?

As previously discussed, we do not believe that readers' advisors should limit their suggestions only to those books they have actually read. If we restricted ourselves this way, we would be suggesting only a limited number of books to readers. Certainly it is important to keep up with popular authors, genres, and trends in fiction. However, to be a good readers' advisor, it is just as important to know both how to think about books and authors and how to talk about them with patrons, as we described earlier in this chapter.

When talking with a patron about a book we have not read, we pick out the elements that indicate the book's appeal to readers. The skills we have mastered in analyzing the books we have read transfer to the more limited information provided by reviews, book jackets, and conversations with patrons. We draw on all these sources to talk about what each book is like and how it fits within a genre. Nothing replaces actually reading a book, assuming we remember in detail everything we have read, but trained readers' advisors can talk comfortably about books they have not read because they can extract and compile useful information from various sources.

We want to stress that there is no shame in admitting we have not read a book; we cannot read everything. In fact, even when they ask if we have read a book, patrons do not necessarily expect us to have read that particular title. They are really asking if it is acceptable for them to take the book. Has anyone read it? We relay any information we have heard about the book from other readers—staff and patrons—or reviews, as well as anything we know about the author or genre. Then we go to the book itself. As we discussed in chapter 3, flipping through a book often tells us whether there is a lot of dialogue, and we can comment on pacing or characterization based on what we discover. We also remind patrons they do not have to read the book if they do not like it. They can come back later or tomorrow, and we will help them find something else.

Best-sellers constitute a special class of book because patrons often ask about them. They want to know what the book is about, so we need to know some particulars of the plot. That information is fairly easy to come by, using resources such as the *New York Times* best-sellers list with its one-sentence annotations, as well as reviews and comments from patrons and colleagues about the book. Since most best-selling authors are repeaters, however, it is also helpful to have, at some point, read at least one typical book by that author. Combining what we know about the current best-seller's plot with our general knowledge of the author, the kind of books he or she writes, and how readers and critics perceive the author, we can readily say enough to satisfy an interested patron.

Suggesting in a genre we are not familiar with is harder. We really need resources: a Popular Fiction List, reference sources, and/or annotated book lists. If we are uncomfortable with Science Fiction, for example, but we get many requests for suggestions from readers, we talk with fans of the genre about their favorites and then have ideas to share with other readers. It behooves us to become familiar with genres popular with our patrons. Just as the only way to answer difficult reference questions is to explore the material and gather aids, so it is in becoming familiar with a genre. There is no quick and easy way to get the job done, but it can be interesting and exciting. We talk more about this activity in chapter 5.

What do we do when we draw a blank?

We've all experienced that familiar sinking feeling when someone asks for something to read—something ostensibly simple, such as a good romance with a little bit of mystery—and nothing comes to mind. At times like these, we have found that the best solution is to go and stand by the books. Walking from our desk to the stacks or a book display seems to get our minds moving, and we are convinced that the books themselves give off an aura. They seem to know we need help and come to our aid. We are amazed at how frequently we will think of a title or an author to fit the situation once we are near the books and handling them. We may be standing at one point in the stacks, when something we see reminds us of a book in another part of the alphabet.

For those skeptical of this approach, remember that *Fiction Catalog* is also a useful resource, especially since it contains descriptions of titles. When we are at a loss for authors or titles to suggest, we look up general topics such as LOVE STORIES, SUSPENSE NOVELS, CHEERFUL STORIES, or HUMOR. Again, an author or title will undoubtedly jog our memory, and we will be able to talk about it with our patron.

In fact, many of the book and electronic resources discussed in chapter 2 can be useful at this point. They serve as memory-joggers that help us get our minds working. They also reinforce with patrons that we are taking their questions seriously. Consulting these resources often helps us start a conversation about books, and that is usually the impetus we need. Once we have overcome the obstacle of finding a book or an author, we are usually able to go on to other suggestions. If not, these reference tools can help us further.

This is also the perfect time to pull out a genre list, such as a Popular Fiction List (*see* the Appendix), if we have one. Patrons may recognize an author they have enjoyed, and readers' advisors will have a list of other popular authors who write in that same genre, although perhaps not in the same style. Annotated book lists can also be a useful resource to give readers. Book lists often will bring to mind a book that can be suggested, and patrons can have a list of all the authors and titles that interest them.

How do we talk about books and authors we personally do not enjoy?

Posted at our readers' advisory desk is *Rosenberg's First Law of Reading: Never apologize for your reading tastes*. We believe that it is important for patrons to feel comfortable in talking with a readers' advisor about any type of book, from so-called trash to classics. Even if we accept this philosophy, however, it does not mean that we will like everything patrons read—and we do not. When a patron asks about an author or a title we personally do not like, we rely on the techniques discussed earlier and talk about what the author does best. What is the strength of the book? What kind of book is it— Intrigue, Romance, Fantasy, Mainstream fiction? What have other readers praised? If we have heard fans of a particular author talk about the book, we share that information with readers. For example, we might say that fans of Stephen King have really liked this book. We may describe the book specifically, if we are familiar with it, or talk generally about the kind of novels the author writes. This approach allows us to speak in nonjudgmental terms, without betraying our personal feelings. We may also talk about an author's popularity and appeal to other readers, again without interjecting our own judgments. It is important to develop some nonjudgmental phrases to employ in situations like this. For example, the author may be "quite a storyteller," or the book may be "a real page-turner" or a "cozy English Village Mystery." A readers' advisor should develop conversational lines that simultaneously respect a patron's taste and leave the advisor's senses of honor and humor intact.

We make a conscientious effort *not* to make negative comments about a book or author. Even if we are certain the reader we are speaking with will understand our intent, a reader who overhears the remarks may not and may be offended. If a new book by a popular author has been poorly reviewed, we might suggest interested readers try it anyway and judge for themselves. If readers have told us they enjoyed a poorly reviewed book, we share that fact with other readers. On the other hand, we might suggest an alternative—an earlier book by the author or a similar title readers have praised.

What do we do when a patron refuses our offer of reading suggestions?

There are times when we cannot *give* book suggestions away, when patrons would not take our suggestions even if we paid them to do so. It happens. Unsatisfactory and discouraging as this situation is to us as readers' advisors, we need to recognize patrons' right to privacy, as well as their right to be made aware of library services. The question is, of course, how can we offer readers' advisory service without seeming to badger readers who enjoy the pleasure of browsing on their own? This takes skill and experience, and staff should work through just what to say. Patrons have a right to decline our help, and both they and we should feel comfortable when they do so. Do not be discouraged by a refusal, or even by a string of rejections. When patrons turn down our offer of book suggestions, we remind them that the service exists and that they should feel comfortable asking for suggestions whenever they are interested. We say, "The staff at this desk are all readers, and we would be glad to offer reading suggestions. Stop by if you ever want some ideas."

How do we handle the question, Can you recommend a good book?

Does any other question strike such fear in a librarian's heart as this? In most cases, we fall back on the interviewing techniques described earlier in this chapter. However, sometimes a patron does not have anything specific in mind or is asking for books for someone else. In both cases, the patron may just want a "good read." This is when we call on standby titles or "sure bets"—books that appeal to a wide range of readers. These are usually titles we have read and enjoyed and can sell by showing our enthusiasm for the book. When we fall back on sure bets, we use them as much to elicit a response from the reader as anything else. Hearing books described, the readers react, either by taking the book or by telling us something else they might enjoy.

The best sure bets are older titles that we can expect to find on the shelves. A current favorite is *Vertical Run*, by Joseph Garber.[7] The novel features a midlevel executive who goes to work one morning to find his boss in his office, waiting to kill him. And his day goes downhill from there. Neither the protagonist nor the reader understands until much later why the hero is attacked at every step by trained assassins. Luckily he was a Green Beret in Vietnam, so his training helps him escape innumerable traps—and set some of his own. This book has proved to be an action-filled, if somewhat violent, read, with its mix of Adventure, Intrigue, and Mystery. Fans of John Grisham have found it very satisfying, despite its lack of legal frame.

The advisor should cultivate sure bets in genres both familiar and personally unexplored. A list of sure bets kept at the advisory desk and updated regularly by staff eliminates the librarian's fear of being unable to remember them. One should be prepared, however, for all the readers who will want to take the list away. The only problem with this strategy is that extra copies of these favorite novels will have to be ordered, because they will rarely be found on the shelf.

How do we suggest books to patrons who have reading restrictions?

We all know the stereotypical little old lady who is supposed to enjoy only gentle English Pastorals but is, in fact, just as likely to read and enjoy a really bloody Serial Murder Suspense novel. It is awkward when readers' advisors make the wrong assumption about a person, and this can be embarrassing both to us and to patrons. More important, it is not fair either to patrons or to readers' advisors to try to outguess readers, or for readers' advisors to try to put restrictions on what we suggest when we have no good reason to believe that restrictions are desired by the reader.

On the other hand, some readers do have restrictions, and they will often voice them during the readers' advisory interview. The restrictions our readers most often mention are sex and violence; as a result, we get requests for "clean" books. This limitation may not be the most common one among your readers, but undoubtedly some limitation will come up. You will want to keep a list of titles that meet your readers' needs and update it whenever you come across titles that fit the criteria.

In dealing with patrons' restrictions, it is also important that we, as readers' advisors and librarians, remain nonjudgmental; it is better not to take sides if a patron is talking on and on about "the terrible state of fiction today," even if we agree. We try to restate patrons' objections in positive terms, reinforcing our position of accepting the entire gamut of reading tastes. For example, we might say, "It sounds as if you're looking for what we call a Gentle Read. Let me give you some authors." The tone we adopt is important; our goal is to meet the needs of *all* readers, not just those who enjoy what we enjoy and who share our prejudices. We need to be aware of differences in attitudes and of how the written word may strike a variety of readers so that our comments inform, not offend. We should also remember the public nature of our readers' advisory interviews. Our comments are easily overheard, and a disparaging remark about an author or type of fiction made to one patron may offend someone else in the area.

As we mentioned above, explicit sex and violence are not the only restrictions readers' advisors encounter. We have readers who prefer only books written by men, and others, only those written by women. One reader likes Spy Thrillers, but only if they take place in the United States. Another wants sea stories, but not those set during World War II. By offering a range of books to readers and by being sensitive to their reactions, we can often help readers identify their own less obvious restrictions and more readily suggest books that appeal to them.

What do we do when readers ask for authors similar to an author we are unfamiliar with?

First, we do not hesitate to admit to the patron that we are not familiar with a particular author. It is better to admit that we have not read everyone than to "fake it" and be found out by the patron. We use lines such as, "I'm not familiar with any of the titles. Can you tell me something about them?" Asking patrons for information often uncovers what they like most about an author and allows us to make decisions about that author's appeal and suggest other, possibly similar authors.

Second, we check for information about the author in reference resources. For instance, is the author on our Popular Fiction List? If so, other authors in the same genre category may appeal to the patron. We also read the entries in the genre reference sources, as well as those in general reference books, looking for clues to traits that will remind us of similar authors or for overt statements of similarities. We will also check electronic sources for suggestions of similar authors.

How do we start a reader on a series?

If the series builds one book on the other, so that readers are lost unless they see the progression, then the only reasonable way to start is with the first book. However, sometimes the first book in a series is not the best choice. For instance, since fictional detectives are often refined by their authors over time, the first book may not be the most representative of the whole series. Once Mystery fans are hooked on a detective series, they will read all the books in the series, but the first one they read has to be right. This same phenomenon is true for series in other genres as well. We always alert the potential reader that we are suggesting a book from a series, and that we are not suggesting the first one, especially since some readers always prefer to read a series in order, no matter what. The rule of thumb we follow is that unless reading the books in the order of their publication is absolutely necessary, we start a reader with the best title we know, no matter where it falls in the series. Several sources are available that list "best" works by an author, and these can help identify titles for advisors who are unfamiliar with the series.

In summary, the readers' advisory interview—basically a conversation between the librarian and the patron about books and reading—is the crux of readers' advisory service. Thus, it is not surprising that extensive preparation and practice are necessary to master the skills involved. Readers' advisors should keep in mind, however, that the goal of the readers' advisory interview is not to get readers to take the books they suggest, but to set up a link between readers and librarians so that patrons see readers' advisory as a library service in the same way that answering reference questions is a library service.

Finally, although the structure of this chapter, and indeed of this entire book, could be seen to imply a step-by-step process through which readers' advisors progress, this is not actually the case. None of us has the time or the opportunity to master all the reference sources and become familiar with the library's fiction collection before we actually encounter patrons and start suggesting books. In fact, learning the many aspects of readers' advisory takes place simultaneously as we work with readers and reference sources. Having become familiar with the techniques described to this point, readers' advisors are now ready to tackle the more involved aspects of readers' advisory discussed in chapter 5.

Notes

1. Duncan Smith to Joyce Saricks, e-mail, February 13, 1996; Kazuo Ishiguro, *The Remains of the Day* (New York: Knopf, 1989).

2. Margaret A. Edwards, *The Fair Garden and the Swarm of Beasts: The Library and the Young Adult,* reprint ed. (Chicago: American Library Assn., 1994), 17–18.

3. Christopher Morley, *Parnassus on Wheels* (Philadelphia: Lippincott, 1917); and Helene Hanff, *84, Charing Cross Road* (Old Tappan, N.J.: Grossman, 1970).

4. Sharon L. Baker, "A Decade's Worth of Research on Browsing Fiction Collections," in *Guiding the Reader to the Next Book,* 130.

5. Philip Shelby, *Days of Drums* (New York: Simon & Schuster, 1996).

6. Ralph Gers and Lillie J. Seward, "Improving Reference Performance: Results of a Statewide Study," *Library Journal* 1 (November 1985): 32–35.

7. Joseph Garber, *Vertical Run* (New York: Bantam, 1995).

5

The Background Readers' Advisors Need in Popular Fiction

Whether a staff of one or part of a team, readers' advisors quickly come to recognize that just reading and talking about books with patrons does not ensure the success of their service. Readers' advisors fare well when they work with readers who share their own reading interests and tastes, but when they happen upon a reader who is interested in an author or a genre they are less familiar with, they realize how necessary it is to have a broad knowledge of popular fiction, even though reference resources may be right at hand.

In this chapter, we discuss in detail the ways in which readers' advisors acquire this knowledge of popular fiction and learn to relate more confidently to a wide range of readers and books. Since familiarity with popular fiction is vital, readers' advisors need to set up a personal reading plan in order to acquaint themselves with genres and authors that are popular with their patrons. In chapter 2, we explained how to use a list such as our Popular Fiction List as a reference tool; in this chapter, we show how, when the list is structured carefully, it can also become a reading list. Next, since readers' advisors need a way to remember information about the books they and other staff members have read, we suggest a format for annotating books. Readers' advisors also need to study genres in depth. We describe this process and examine the rewards such studies bring to readers' advisors.

Designing a Reading Plan

To be conversant with the types of popular fiction patrons request, readers' advisors need a broad background in popular fiction. We designed our library's Popular Fiction List to serve both as a reference tool and as a reading outline that would help acquaint us with authors in the genres our patrons frequently request. The Appendix shows the Popular Fiction List used in our library in the winter of 1997. You may not need a list as formally structured as ours to develop a reading plan, but some sort of basic list of authors is a necessity. Using information gained by identifying the reading public's tastes and creating a list of popular genres and authors, we readers' advisors can structure our reading in a way that helps familiarize us with the genres and authors that readers consistently request. Such a list provides advisors with the foundation on which to build a reading plan—a place to begin as we work to familiarize ourselves with the fiction that is popular in our collections. This list must be comprehensive enough to provide a broad overview of each genre popular in the library, yet narrow enough to allow the readers' advisor to begin to understand the appeal of both the genre and representative authors without undertaking an unrealistic reading program.

Detailed suggestions for compiling a list of popular authors were presented in chapter 2. Once the list has been developed, it can help in assessing personal and staff reading strengths and in the consequent development of suitable reading plans. After writing their initials by the names of authors they have read, staff can identify the genres in which they have read the least and concentrate on these unfamiliar areas, beginning with those most popular with patrons. A good way to start is for each readers' advisor to set a goal of reading a certain number of authors in an unfamiliar genre, one typical title per author, within a set time period. It is useful to set a formal time for discussing the reading and the conclusions drawn about the author's appeal with a supervisor or another reader. That may not always be possible, but it is important that all staff keep reading fiction to expand their knowledge of authors, titles, and genres popular with patrons. Since titles are not included on our Popular Fiction List, experienced readers' advisors must rely on reference sources, as well as discussion with patrons and other staff, to identify which authors from the list to read first and then to discover a representative title by each author.

Discussion of the titles read is an important element in this exercise. Figure 5.1, Suggested Discussion Questions, offers examples of

Figure 5.1
Suggested Discussion Questions

---

1. What does the author do best?
2. Does the book/author emphasize characters or story more?
3. Do you fall into the book immediately or learn the story and characters at a more leisurely pace?
4. Is there an especially detailed background, full of those fascinating extra details we find in some books? (For example, there are details of archaeology, nineteenth-century Egypt, and the status of women in Elizabeth Peters's Amelia Peabody mystery series. See chapter 3 for further explanation.)
5. What other authors/titles does the book remind you of (not subject but feel and appeal)?
6. Who else might enjoy reading the book and why? (For example, someone who likes Adventure novels? Puzzles? Strong characters? An interesting setting? Action? Or a Gentle Read?)
7. If it is a genre book, how does it fit in that genre?
8. What makes the book popular?
9. Why do readers like the book? Have you overheard or picked up comments about the title or author?

---

the kinds of questions important to consider in both reading and talking about these books. The questions draw heavily on the nature of appeal, as discussed in chapter 3, but they also direct advisors toward techniques that can help them share the appeal information they discover with patrons. As readers' advisors become comfortable with questions such as these and the thought patterns they reflect, we can use variations of them to question readers and to extract information about the kinds of books that might appeal to them. These questions also help us think about books and appeal in ways that make discovering similar authors easier. For example, reading Jacquelyn Mitchard's *The Deep End of the Ocean* reminded more than one readers' advisor of the thought-provoking, elegantly written novels of Rosellen Brown *(Before and After)* and Jane Hamilton

(A Map of the World).[1] Although not linked by subject, these books reflect similarities in writing quality, and all feature strong characterizations in their stories of how families cope with tragic events. These are the kinds of connections that readers appreciate and that a thoughtful directed reading plan teaches readers' advisors to make.

In addition to formal discussions with one or more staff members, there should be other formal and informal channels of discussion so that everyone may share some of their discoveries about the titles they have been reading. One formal opportunity to share is through written annotations of the books read, a technique we will discuss in the next section. These annotations should be shared with staff members in addition to being made available for the public. A time set aside to discuss books at staff meetings can provide another opportunity, as can the informal discussions among staff that we stressed in chapter 4. Sharing information about authors and titles helps all staff doing readers' advisory: It expands our background and helps us make useful connections between authors more readily. There is also a particular pleasure in sharing newfound titles and authors that is contagious and is then passed on easily from staff to patrons.

In some cases, only one or two staff members may be providing readers' advisory service in a library, and they may not be part of a department that has readers' advisory as a defined responsibility. If you are in this situation, do not be deterred; developing and working through a reading list is a useful activity no matter how few people are involved. Individual readers' advisors should attack the Popular Fiction List in the same way that a team of advisors does, i.e., by starting with the genres that are most popular with their patrons.

As we discuss the value of reading and establishing a reading plan, it is important to acknowledge a question that is often raised: How much reading is required to be a successful readers' advisor? Since looking for appeal is primarily an intellectual exercise, it is important to acknowledge that there is more than one way to go about this activity successfully. Some of us feel that we must read several books before we are comfortably certain of the appeal of an author or genre; others feel they can read fewer titles and work with reviews, book jackets, reference materials, and readers' comments in order to ascertain the appeal. Both approaches are sound. Our feeling is that when readers' advisors have reached a certain level of expertise, we should have a sense of how much primary material we personally need to read, and we should be able to balance our reading and research patterns accordingly. Whether readers' advisors read numerous books or just representative titles, we will certainly need to rely on other sources; in fact, we learn to pull information from every source available in order to clearly discern an author's appeal to the reader.

A thoughtfully constructed and current Popular Fiction List provides an invaluable resource for readers' advisors. It lays the foundation for an individual or group-directed reading plan and can be the basis for advanced genre study, discussed later in this chapter.

Writing Annotations

Although developing a reading list and basing a conscientious reading program on that list is a logical starting place for gaining popular fiction expertise, it is only the first step. Reading and talking about books are not enough unless some written record is also kept, for without a written record it is difficult to retain the impressions and insights that were gained when the books were fresh in our minds.

Writing annotations—formalized descriptions of books we have read—is one way to keep track of what is being read and, more important, what is being learned about the appeal of the books read. These annotations are not meant to be critical reviews; but they should delineate the appeal of the book and how the title is related to other titles and authors, as well as provide other information, such as a plot summary, that potential readers and readers' advisors may need. Once the information is in written form, it can be made available to others, whether they are staff working with readers or the readers themselves.

We have changed our annotation form over the years, but we still follow an established format for every annotation to ensure consistency. (*See* Figure 5.2 for the annotation format we use and Figure 5.3 for a sample annotation.) Our annotations are typed on a computer; printed copies are then put on five-by-eight-inch index cards and kept in a file box for perusal by patrons. Copies are also added to a data base for electronic retrieval. We include the following bibliographic information: author, title, publication date, and number of pages. Including the publication date and the number of pages has proved quite useful because some people like to read only contemporary fiction, and a surprising number of people base their book selection, at least in part, on length.

Figure 5.2
Annotation Format

AUTHOR:

TITLE:

PUBLICATION DATE:

NUMBER OF PAGES:

GEOGRAPHICAL SETTING:

TIME PERIOD:

SERIES:

PLOT SUMMARY:

SUBJECT HEADINGS:

APPEAL:

SIMILAR AUTHORS:

NAME:

We have a set location on our form to record the novel's geographical setting and time period. Having this information in one place saves time when we are looking for English Mysteries, Medieval Romances, etc. The time period is noted as present, future, or the particular historical period. In order to ensure uniformity, we use historical periods based on *Fiction Catalog*'s Titles and Subject Index.

Figure 5.3
Sample annotation

AUTHOR: Findley, Timothy

TITLE: Headhunter

PUBLICATION DATE: 1994

NUMBER OF PAGES: 440 p.

GEOGRAPHICAL SETTING: Toronto

TIME PERIOD: near future

SERIES: NA

PLOT SUMMARY: In this homage to Joseph Conrad's *Heart of Darkness,* ex-librarian Lilah Kemp releases Kurtz from the confines of that book, and Toronto becomes the dark and fetid jungle in which Kurtz is stalked by a modern Marlow. This near-future Toronto of nightmares is polluted—both the physical environment and the souls of the inhabitants—and gangs and a mysterious plague run rampant. Moving from art galleries to psychiatric hospitals to elegant homes to men's pornography clubs, Marlow hunts Kurtz and the evil he represents. Multiple interwoven plot lines (involving, among others, characters based on Emma Bovary, Jay Gatsby, and Dickens's Fagin) are all connected at the nexus of the Parkin Institute, which Kurtz heads.

SUBJECT HEADINGS: Psychological Novels; Psychiatry; Psychiatric Hospitals; Psychiatrists; Schizophrenics; Librarians; Dystopias; Plagues; Spiritualists; Artists; Art Galleries; Sisters; Blackmail; Child Pornography; Suicide; Murder; Power; Good versus Evil; Madness; Disease; Animal Experimentation; Conrad, Joseph, *Heart of Darkness*

SIMILAR AUTHORS: Piercy, Marge; Atwood, Margaret

APPEAL: menacing atmosphere; densely written; eccentric characters; bleak; philosophical; hard-edged; evocative; foreboding; detailed setting; poetic; elegant; multiple plot lines; issue oriented; thought provoking; character centered;

NAME: Joyce Saricks

In another section, we record series information, using character names or actual series names to identify books that are linked. Many of our readers are fans of series; in fact, they may only know books by the series character rather than author or title, so it is important to be able to retrieve this information.

We also include a subject headings section and have discovered the need for a thesaurus of subject headings, which everyone consults. We rely on *Fiction Catalog* subject headings, as well as those used by Hennepin County on Carl Corporation's *NoveList*. Subject headings are assigned only if they are an important access point to the book. For example, we might assign the subject heading COLLEGE AND UNIVERSITY LIFE if the reader would get a feel for life on a college campus while reading the book, but not if the only connection is that the story happens to be set on a college campus. Assigning subject headings forces annotators to look at the book in terms of what might interest a potential reader. However, since headings also provide an access point when we are searching for a book a patron—or someone on the staff—remembers reading, but for which we have no bibliographic information, we try to assign a range of headings that might be useful retrieval points. We also include genre designations, such as Mystery Stories, Westerns, and Romantic Suspense, in the subject heading list.

A feature that makes our annotations unique is the inclusion of a place to list similar authors and, sometimes, specific similar titles. Determining similar authors requires annotators to place the books in the readers' context and to think of other authors and titles with the same appeal, as we discussed in chapter 3. By looking in the similar author listing, a patron or readers' advisor who wants other books "just like" an annotated author can find suggestions. This is one of the real advantages of devising a system that is available to patrons. Readers find it very satisfying to flip through our file of annotation cards looking for their favorite authors and then to follow up on the suggestions given in the similar authors section.

The plot summary should reveal enough of the story to entice a reader without giving away any details the author did not intend the reader to know ahead of time. Our descriptions indicate why a certain book appeals to readers and give the readers' advisor enough information to discuss the book. These annotation/plot summaries differ from the briefer, more directed annotations used on annotated book lists and discussed in chapter 6. We put no stipulation on length, but all staff understand the importance of avoiding involved summaries. Most important, these annotations are written for readers, to provide them with enough information to help them decide if they might want to read a book. *Sequels* by Janet and Jonathan Husband, is a good place to study annotations written for readers.[2] Their characterizations of authors set a standard to emulate, as they show how to describe authors in terms of their appeal to fans. Also helpful is Margaret Edwards' *The Fair Garden and a Swarm of Beasts: The Library and the Young Adult*, which has a section on annotation writing.[3]

In addition, in the plot summary section we also mention any style and plot elements not specifically included in the summary— comments about dialect, for example, and sidelights (e.g., "fascinating details about Chippendale antiques," "intriguing discussion between the atheist wife and minister husband," "descriptions of day-to-day life in a medieval monastery," or "extensive maps included"). These notes are not simply repetitions of the subject headings; rather, they give annotators an opportunity to expand on the headings. We also try to indicate features that may limit a book's appeal, if we have not already worked this information into the annotation itself. As we mentioned before in discussing the readers' advisory interview, we have found that some novels have characteristics a considerable number of our readers want to be made aware of. Whenever possible, we try to convey that information in the plot summary section of the annotation, using non-judgmental phrases that make readers aware of topics or forms of presentation, such as stream of consciousness, that may not appeal to them. None of our annotations or book suggestions comes with a guarantee of safety, and the occasional strong word or violent scene will not necessarily put off a reader who prefers more gentle works. On the other hand, if strong language or violence or sex, however limited, affect the tone of the book or stand out as a glaring or shocking intrusion, this should be noted. There should also be a universal understanding among annotators of when this issue should be addressed. We advise that the practice of noting elements that limit the appeal of novels be used sparingly and judiciously, and only when readers in sufficient numbers make it clear that they desire this information. Indicating the presence of such elements in the annotation can be quite straightforward. Phrases such as "steamy sex" in the summary itself suggest the content of the novel and warn readers who may prefer something gentler. The content of the annotation in Figure 5.3, for example, implies that this is not a book for the faint of heart.

We have recently begun adding appeal terms to our annotations as well, and we are compiling a thesaurus of these terms. In developing this list, we discovered that appeal terms tend to be adjectives, in contrast to subject headings, which are always nouns. In our annotations, appeal elements are occasionally listed with the noun for clarity, as in "eccentric characters" or "menacing atmosphere." While subject headings are more objective and straightforward, appeal terms are frequently subjective; they reflect the more subjective nature of readers' advisory and respond to readers' requests and moods in a way that transcends the limitations of subject headings. Adding these appeal terms, just as we apply subject headings, provides staff and readers who use the annotations access points that address the "feel" of the book, not merely its content.

No matter what format is employed by a library, we suggest that every readers' advisory staff develop a formalized annotation system with which they feel comfortable. You may not need or want to list everything we include in ours, or you may feel that you require information we have not mentioned. Whatever the case, every library that is serious about doing readers' advisory work should develop a method of recording what the staff is reading in a way that allows retrieval of the information when it is needed. All readers' advisors should be required to write a set number of annotations. We require at least two written annotations a month from all of our staff, although most staff members read and annotate well beyond that number. Putting anything into writing forces us to concentrate on using precisely the right words. Annotators also focus on the book's appeal and thus take a good look at the title as it compares to others in the collection and to readers' tastes.

In order to keep track of appeal information about a book as we are reading it, we use a special form, shown in Figure 5.4, as a bookmark. Printed on $8^{1}/_{2}$-by-11-inch sheets, this book summary, which complements our annotation format, allows us to record our first impressions while they are fresh in our minds. We simply jot down, under each of the appeal characteristics, thoughts as they strike us while reading. These notes can be expanded later when we actually write our annotations. Keeping these notes helps us capture valuable details and impressions we might otherwise miss or forget. When we finish a book, we may also consult the appeal questions covered in chapter 3 (Figures 3.1 through 3.4) since they help us focus on specific appeal elements as they relate to that book. When we consider the book in light of these elements, we can better focus and organize our impressions. Whether we actually annotate each book or not, we keep these book sheets in personal notebooks for reference. They often prove invaluable when we are trying to remember more about a book we read, are putting together a list of books on a particular subject or with a specific appeal, or are

Figure 5.4
Book Summary Format

AUTHOR: DATE READ:

TITLE: PUB. DATE:

GENRE: PAGES:

APPEAL CHARACTERISTICS: PLOT SUMMARY:

    PACING

    CHARACTERIZATIONS

    STORY LINE   Geographical setting:

                      Time period:

    FRAME
                      Series:

SIMILAR AUTHORS: Subject headings:

---

participating in a genre study and want to refresh our memories of books we have read in that genre.

Although writing annotations may seem like a lot of work, the effort is worthwhile for both readers' advisors who write the annotations and the staff and patrons who use them for reference and reading suggestions. As already mentioned, writing the annotations makes a readers' advisor focus on the aspects of the books that appeal to readers, and these are the same elements readers' advisors need in talking with readers. In time, this ability to summarize is naturally carried over to books that one reads but does not annotate, as experienced readers' advisors unconsciously annotate books they are reading. Nothing equals actually writing book annotations, however, and even the most experienced readers' advisors need to continue annotating books they read.

Studying a Genre

Over time, we realized that in-depth studies of individual genres were absolutely essential. At first we looked primarily at individual titles for their appeal elements. Then we began to set up groupings of authors and titles that we discovered had similar appeal for our readers, and we started to create lists in the pattern of "If you like, . . ." discussed in detail in chapter 6.

We still use this procedure when we come upon an author for whom there apparently are no similar authors. For example, in an attempt to satisfy Danielle Steel's numerous fans, we recently updated our "If you like Danielle Steel" bookmark. On our service desk we taped a note that listed general appeal characteristics for Steel's books—women's problems novels (which deal with family and relationships, disease, and/or career problems), soap opera in tone, fast-paced, stereotypical characters we relate to from the first page, a strong main character whose point of view permeates the novel and who triumphs in the end, and a romantic feel—and allowed space to list books that might appeal to Steel's fans. Titles such as LaVyrle Spencer's *That Camden Summer*, Katherine Stone's *Pearl Moon*, and Barbara Delinsky's *Together Alone* were added to the sheet, along with other titles we had come upon through our reading of books and reviews, as well as from our conversations with patrons.[4] By using this process, we have greatly increased our knowledge of the appeal of these blockbuster authors. In addition, we have created thoughtful appeal-based lists, not available elsewhere, of similar novelists and titles for popular authors such as John Grisham.

Although we have been pleased with the useful lists we have created and the way in which we have refined our knowledge of an author's appeal for the reader, we have, unfortunately, had to start pretty much from scratch each time. Therefore, rather than just reacting to the current popular authors one at a time, we realized that we needed to look at a larger unit. We thought that if we expanded this process of identifying individual author characteristics and similarities to a whole genre, we would be well on our way to an understanding of popular fiction based on the attraction it had for the reader. We decided to concentrate individually on each of the fiction genres on our Popular Fiction List. Based on our experience in working with a single author, we expected the following results from genre study: a basic understanding of the characteristics and pattern of the genre, a clearer picture of the appeal of the genre, a greater familiarity with the range of authors in that genre, a sense of which authors appeal to the same readers, the ability to communicate better with readers of the genre, and increased staff comfort levels when dealing with unfamiliar genres. Such a study would direct our energies.

In studying each genre, we first tried to identify the standardized pattern, the rules for constructing plot and characters, that structures each genre. We theorized that if we could understand the pattern, we would have a hint as to the appeal of the genre. We asked some of the same questions regarding story line, characterization, frame, and pacing that we used when looking for the appeal elements in individual books. We began by brainstorming these characteristics. First, we asked about what common characteristics books in a particular genre share. We could establish fairly quickly, for example, the fact that Romances all seem to revolve around a romantic relationship and end happily; Mysteries have a body and a detective/crime solver; Suspense novels have characters placed in jeopardy, and so forth. We would consider the same appeal issues discussed in chapter 3 and apply them more generally to the genre as a whole, rather than to individual titles. As might be expected, we found this to be an intellectually challenging and very satisfying activity. An example of this process and the results of such a study, Figure 5.5 shows the final revision of the list of genre characteristics from our study of Suspense. The connection between the characteristics, which reveal the pattern of the genre, and the appeal elements described in chapter 3 is readily apparent in this schema, with each characteristic relating to a specific appeal element: pacing, characterization, story line, and frame.

When we first embarked on a genre study, we selected Thrillers, a genre that was in great demand; fortunately, it was also one many staff members already read and enjoyed. As we looked at genre reference material, we tried to identify the elements and the pattern of the genre that made it so popular. We found that, with a little extrapolation, both the "Themes and Types" section of Betty Rosenberg's first edition of *Genreflecting* and books about writing genre fiction, such as Dean R. Koontz's *Writing Popular Fiction*, were particularly helpful in understanding the traditional genres.[5] We also often picked up some useful information from the introductory material contained in genre reference books. (See chapter 2 for more information on reference sources.) We did a lot of reading, talking, and brainstorming as we tried to identify the elements that make the genre as a whole so appealing and to determine a preliminary list of characteristics.

We found that as we identified the pattern and appeal of a particular genre, we could use this information right away in our

Figure 5.5
Characteristics of the Suspense Genre

GENERAL CHARACTERISTICS

1. Action takes place within a narrow time frame, often a matter of days.

2. Reader identifies with the protagonist and feels the same danger. But the reader often follows the antagonist's thoughts and actions, too, and thus knows more than the protagonist.

3. Story usually follows the same pattern, with unexpected danger from an unknown source intruding into the protagonist's life. The resolution is brought about through a confrontation between the hero/heroine and villain, and the protagonist always survives.

4. Dark, menacing atmosphere is essential and underscores the danger to the protagonist. As the story unfolds, tension pervades, and the reader has a sense of uneasiness, uncertainty, even before the protagonist senses anything is wrong.

SOFTER-EDGED SUSPENSE

1. Bodies are usually offstage and are not clinically described.

2. Although the protagonist is often stalked by the villain, there is more threatened danger, atmosphere, building of emotions. Suspense is generated more by atmosphere than action.

3. Protagonist is often a woman who is resourceful and who saves herself in the end. Police may be present but often play a smaller role in the final confrontation.

4. Details are more likely to relate to descriptions of characters than to crimes.

5. Roller-coaster pacing follows a pattern of building and then easing up, only to build again.

Benchmark author: Mary Higgins Clark *(A Stranger Is Watching)*

Typical authors:

　　Michael Allegretto *(The Watchmen)*

　　Marjorie Dorner *(Freeze Frame)*

　　Joy Fielding *(The Deep End)*

　　Paula Gosling *(Fair Game)*

　　Jonellen Heckler *(Circumstances Unknown)*

　　Marilyn Wallace *(The Seduction)*

HARD-EDGED SUSPENSE

1. More details of crimes and police procedures. Protagonist is often a detective and may or may not be in immediate danger, but may be working against time to protect someone else.

2. More graphic descriptions, often including sexual situations, physical violence, and strong language.

3. Suspense is generated more through action than atmosphere.

4. Relentless pace—stays in high gear throughout the novel.

Benchmark author: Thomas Harris *(The Red Dragon)*

Typical authors:

Robert L. Duncan *(Serpent's Mark)*

Andrew Klavan *(Don't Say a Word)*

Herbert Lieberman *(Shadow Dancer)*

John Sandford *(Rules of Prey)*

Derek Van Arman *(Just Killing Time)*

David Wiltse *(Close to the Bone*

---

readers' advisory interviews. For example, if a reader told us he liked books in which a tourist or other innocent character was unexpectedly caught up in a situation involving spies and international intrigue, we knew he would be unlikely to enjoy Ian Fleming's novels of superhero James Bond but might very well be satisfied with novels by someone like Helen MacInnes. When we finished Thrillers and embarked on Mysteries, we recognized early on that most Mysteries are dominated by the character of the detective or problem solver and that much of their appeal revolves around that character's personality. Using this observation, we began to ask readers seeking Mystery Stories to describe the main character of the Mystery series they enjoyed. A reader who described little old ladies who stumbled upon cases wanted quite different books from one who described hard-boiled detectives. Then we compared this information to our own mental list of types of detectives and could suggest authors who used similar detectives.

Extending the pattern we used when working with individual authors, we picked one of the most popular authors in the Thriller genre and read some typical titles by that author. We compared the novels we read with what we felt was the pattern and appeal of the whole genre. We identified the most prominent appeal elements— attitude of the main character, pacing, setting, etc. When we were studying Thrillers, Robert Ludlum was the premier Thriller writer and was enormously popular in our library. Thus, we read his Thrillers, looking for their appeal, and we were able to identify several elements that were evident in the majority of his books: strong male characters with extraordinary training and stamina, who operate under a personal moral code; fast-paced plots with many sudden twists and turns; frequent and graphic violence; and international settings.

Every Thriller may have some of these characteristics, but novels with Ludlum's appeal usually contain this specific combination of features. After identifying the Ludlum appeal elements, we continued looking at other well-known and frequently read authors in the genre and compared them with Ludlum: Did they have the same elements or something different? Which Thriller authors also appealed to Ludlum fans? Did they share the same elements? Naturally, we also found Thriller writers who did not appeal to Ludlum fans. For instance, John le Carré's central male characters certainly possess personal moral codes and superior intellectual powers, but many of our Ludlum fans did not like le Carré. By reading le Carré, as well as about him, and talking with his fans, we decided that John le Carré has a dark quality and a slower, more measured pacing that is not typical of the more action-packed Ludlum-type novel. The difference does not mean that we would never suggest a le Carré novel to Ludlum readers, but it is unlikely that we would suggest him to readers who tell us they read Ludlum for his energetic pacing. The next step, then, was to follow the same pattern in order to compile a list of Thrillers with le Carré's pacing and style for his many fans.

And so the process was repeated for the most-asked-for authors. Most popular Thriller writers could be placed in one of the five groupings we had tentatively identified, each one with its own unique appeal elements. These were as follows:

Action—Robert Ludlum, benchmark

Superhero—Ian Fleming and John Gardner's James Bond, benchmarks

Cynical Realism—John le Carré, benchmark

Amateur/Adventure—Helen MacInnes, benchmark

Technology—Tom Clancy, benchmark

Defining the characteristics of these subgroupings or subgenres in exact yet nonexclusive terms is often very difficult; we are still grappling with this issue. Defining subgenres is useful in helping us classify the rapidly growing body of information we are learning about the genre. We may sense that a set of novels has the same appeal, but putting that appeal into words is often very challenging. When we did succeed in creating and defining a grouping, we could use the terms decided upon, not only in our own discussions with colleagues but with readers as well, and this proved very satisfying. Patrons also began to reflect and repeat the new terminology, and they quickly showed us where we did not have quite the right idea. For example, when talking with Tom Clancy fans, we might ask if the technical detail is the feature they most appreciate. Since we know Clancy and the Techno-Thriller subgenre, we know this is one of the features that separates this subgenre from others. If the patrons respond that they do read Clancy for the technical detail, other authors, such as Dale Brown and Craig Thomas, who also include many technical military details, may be good suggestions. Sometimes readers respond that they read these books for another feature, perhaps strong characterizations, an integral element of the Cynical Realism subgenre. Understanding the subgenres and asking readers questions based on our knowledge can lead to more satisfying readers' advisory interactions, for us as well as for patrons.

We have learned through experience that none of these subgroupings is mutually exclusive. From working with readers and their varied interests, we know there is crossover among subgenres, just as there is among genres, based on what readers say they enjoy and are in the mood to read. For example, Figure 5.5 identifies two major subgenres in the Suspense genre and lists characteristics and typical authors for each. These are opposite ends of the spectrum, and the authors range from softer- to harder-edged Suspense. While the Harris readers may not read Mary Higgins Clark, they may enjoy others on the softer-edged list. A title like C. Terry Cline's *Reaper*, for example, is a little harder edged than Clark's books and is thus read by some fans of both Clark and Harris.[6] Identifying subgenres and thinking of authors in terms of narrower groups with set characteristics makes gaining an understanding of the genre and where authors generally fit into it much easier. This understanding helps us see the appeal characteristics that allow us to take readers across genres or subgenres. We need to know subgenres but not be limited by them.

Figure 5.6 outlines how to conduct a genre study. In addition, we have some guidelines to share, drawn from our experience leading and participating in genre studies over the last ten years. First, genre studies take time. We allow about two years to study a genre in order to have time to read extensively, to discuss the genre and representative authors among ourselves and with patrons, and to reflect on our discoveries and draw conclusions. In his book *An Aesthetics of Junk Fiction*, Thomas J. Roberts discusses a comment from James Gunn, professor, editor, and writer of Science Fiction, who says, basically, that to know a genre, one needs to read about a hundred books.[7] It takes that much reading not only "to acquire the internal map of the genre" needed to read pleasurably but also to understand that a story fits the basic pattern of the genre or does something new, to be able to recognize creaking reworkings of genre conventions, as opposed to innovation. Vast as this number may seem, it is probably accurate if we are exploring a genre on our own.

Genre study, however, should not be a solitary activity. That is the second guideline. We really need at least one other person

Figure 5.6
Tips for Studying a Genre

1. Select a high-demand genre—one that staff reads and enjoys.
2. Gather resources to gain an overview of the genre (reference books as well as staff knowledge).
3. Make a preliminary list of the genre's appeal characteristics and pattern; note possible subgenres.
4. Identify the benchmark/most popular author, in general and for each subgenre. What characterizes that author's books?
5. Read other authors in the genre. Do they fit with the benchmark, or are they different? How?
6. Formulate a list of appeal characteristics of the whole genre. Define subgenres with their own unique list of characteristics and representative authors.

reading and reacting to reap benefits. While our department is always engaged in a genre study, we know of other librarians, often those in smaller libraries, who participate in genre studies with staff from other area libraries. We could even do this by e-mail or telephone, although the personal contact when sharing books would be missing. By participating with others in a genre study, we receive the benefit of having read the hundred books, without actually having read more than two to three dozen over a two-year period. While some reading is absolutely essential to discover the appeal of authors and the genre as a whole, readers' advisors, as we have said earlier, are trained to glean information from a variety of sources, and genre studies provide an opportunity to practice those skills.

Third, although we read and discuss books as we explore a genre, we do not discuss them in the same way we might in a book discussion. We are reading to discover the book, author, and genre's appeal to fans. We are not reading for plot but to discover why the author and genre are so popular. Our discussion reflects this emphasis. We focus on the following: How do these authors and titles fit with others in this genre? Which of these authors are similar and fit together in subgenres? What do the books we read suggest about the appeal of the genre as a whole? What do readers tell us about these authors and others they enjoy? These discussions help us focus our thoughts and discoveries, and the results of them direct our future reading. For example, the group might consider questions such as those listed in Figure 5.7 for a discussion of Sue Grafton and other female Private Investigators. It is easy to see how such questions focus the discussion and lead to conclusions about a particular author as well as genre and subgenre.

Fourth, in an organized genre study, one person should be designated as the leader to direct the reading and focus the discussion. Preferably, this should be a person who knows something about the genre, but fans need to be careful not to skew the reading list and discussion only toward aspects they enjoy. This leader reads widely, gathers resources about the genre, determines reading assignments, and helps the group draw conclusions.

Fifth, in determining which genre to study first, select a genre popular both with readers and with the librarians studying it. This is not to say that it is not important to study genres the staff does not personally enjoy, but do not begin the process of studying genres by choosing one that is unfamiliar and/or unpopular. We speak from experience in saying that it is very difficult to keep up enthusiasm for an unpopular genre and very difficult to understand why

Figure 5.7
Questions to Consider in Discussing Sue Grafton and
Authors of Female Private Investigator Mysteries

1. What characteristics/appeal elements do these books
   illustrate?
2. Why are these Mysteries so popular?

   Immediacy of first-person narration?

   Likable protagonist?

   Series character?

   Lower level of violence?

   Social and moral issues inherent in her cases?

   Step-by-step investigation (as opposed to the "snooping"
      in many cozies)?

   Sense of place?

   Self-reliance of the protagonist?
3. What is the difference between Grafton's books and Private
   Investigator mysteries and Police Procedural Mysteries that feature women characters, such as those by Lillian O'Donnell? Would
   fans of Grafton also like these or other Police
   Procedurals?
4. Who is Grafton's audience? Women or Men? Does the sex of the
   author (and the P.I.) make a difference?

readers enjoy it. Start with a genre participants read and enjoy; they
will be more comfortable reading widely and sharing their knowledge of books already read, and they will have a wider array of
familiar authors to draw upon. Later, when participants are familiar
with the techniques and benefits of a genre study, move on to more
difficult, less familiar genres.

Finally, we have some more specific suggestions related to the
organization of a genre study group.

1. In making reading assignments, have everyone read at least one
   specific title together, rather than many different titles. Then
   everyone has the same frame of reference to draw on in discussing that author and title. If three books are being read for a

two-month period, we might assign two specific titles and allow one free choice by a similar author. (For example, in reading female Private Investigators, we might assign titles by Sue Grafton and Marcia Muller, plus one other similar female investigator of the reader's choice.) We encourage participants to read widely in the genre, beyond those authors and titles assigned, but by assigning specific titles and encouraging participants to draw on reader opinions for suggestions of other authors to read, we both focus on known works and force ourselves to talk with readers about other authors they enjoy.

2. Talk about the genre with staff and patrons. As we said earlier, genre study is a another example of readers' advisory as a cooperative activity. Talking with staff—all staff, not just those who work with fiction—and readers forces us to put our thoughts and discoveries into words, and readers either affirm or redirect our conclusions. In addition, all genre study makes us more conscious of pattern and appeal in all genres, not just in the genre we are studying. Genre study focuses us on appeal and the concept of similar authors; it reinforces the nature of the readers' advisory interview. We do better readers' advisory when we draw on our expanded understanding of genre fiction and share our enthusiasm with other readers.

3. Organize monthly or bimonthly meetings. A genre study is a commitment of time to read and reflect and of time to meet and discuss. Regular meetings allow participants to share their discoveries of current reading as well as to fit them together with authors read previously.

4. Read widely and follow up on suggestions from staff and patrons. The leader, especially, needs both to read ahead of the group and to remain flexible enough to change direction if the discussion warrants this.

One question we are frequently asked is what kind of product a staff can expect at the conclusion of a genre study. Obviously, from an administrative point of view, a commitment of two years to extensive reading and discussion should produce something that reflects all the hard work. In addition to the greatly increased understanding of the genre and the ability to work with readers and fans of genre fiction in general, other products can be created. One possibility is a schema of the genre. Figure 5.5 shows such a schema for the Suspense genre, with general characteristics of that genre followed by those of the two subgenres identified in the study, along with typical authors in each.

Another product might be a bookmark or book list. When we studied Suspense, we were able to update two very popular bookmarks, "If you read Mary Higgins Clark's Novels of Suspense, try one of these" and "If you read Thomas Harris's Novels of Suspense, try one of these," with appropriate lists of authors and titles we had discovered in our reading. Our study of Historical Fiction led to a popular annotated book list, with each of us contributing three or four annotations of books we had read during the study. Tangible products can be a relatively straightforward result of a genre study, but they should not be our focus. We study genres to expand our knowledge and skills. The time and effort we invest are far more than that needed to develop bookmarks and book lists, and the results of genre studies are more far-reaching.

The plan for a genre study we present and pursue requires time and energy. We realize it may seem intimidating; it may sound like so much work that it is not worth even trying. But *all* directed reading helps readers' advisors work better with patrons. Smaller steps, such as those described above in Designing a Reading Plan, send us in the right direction and may inspire us to participate in more ambitious reading plans, such as those for genre studies. Whatever genre reading we do, we will gain a greater awareness of the authors and their appeal to readers. We begin to see the pattern that a genre follows; we see links between similar authors. We learn quickly when we embark on any reading program that, with our heightened and directed perceptions, we more readily uncover links and useful information in books we have read about or heard about, as well as in those we read or skim.

Whenever readers' advisors undertake a genre study, the benefits are immediate. We quickly improve our ability to identify the appeal of genres and to recognize where new authors fit within them. We gain confidence in our ability to work with a wide range of readers, as many of our patrons are genre readers. Genre studies are particularly helpful in making staff more comfortable with less familiar genres. Studying a genre allows readers' advisors to gain a kind of control over our expanding knowledge of popular fiction, to refine our ability to define a genre and the groupings within it, and to apply what we learn about one genre to others. We see genre study as an ongoing pursuit, one that is perhaps neverending but is certainly rewarding and stimulating.

The thinking processes described in this chapter evolve as reader' advisors work more and more closely with readers. As readers' advisors become more skilled, we initiate activities that help us provide better service and that continue to challenge us intellectually. We also begin to realize that in printed reference sources we cannot find all the information we need to help readers, and we therefore begin to create our own tools. As we pointed out, our Popular Fiction List came about in just this way and remains a source of authors to read to broaden readers' advisors' backgrounds in genre fiction and, in its revising, serves as an exercise in analyzing the current genre interests of readers who use our library. A book annotation system is another example of the kinds of tools readers' advisors develop. Analyses of the appeal of certain books to the reader and of individual genres provide readers' advisors with intellectual tools of a sort, with a framework that allows readers' advisors to work both in greater depth and with more ease in helping readers find books that interest them.

Notes

1. Jacquelyn Mitchard, *The Deep End of the Ocean* (New York: Viking, 1996); Rosellen Brown, *Before and After* (New York: Farrar, 1992); and Jane Hamilton, *A Map of the World* (New York: Doubleday, 1994).
2. Husband and Husband, *Sequels*.
3. Edwards, *The Fair Garden*, 128–30.
4. LaVyrle Spencer, *That Camden Summer* (New York: Putnam, 1996); Katherine Stone, *Pearl Moon* (New York: Columbine, 1995); and Barbara Delinsky, *Together Alone* (New York: HarperCollins, 1995).
5. Betty Rosenberg, "Themes and Types," in *Genreflecting* (appears at the end of each chapter) (Littleton, Colo.: Libraries Unlimited, 1982); Dean R. Koontz, *Writing Popular Fiction* (Cincinnati: Writer's Digest, 1972).
6. C. Terry Cline, *Reaper* (New York: D. I. Fine, 1989).
7. Thomas J. Roberts, *An Aesthetics of Junk Fiction* (Athens, Ga.: Univ. of Georgia Pr., 1990), 213–14.

6 Promotion

I n this chapter, we discuss some activities that promote readers' advisory service. While many of these activities can be used for other, equally valid purposes, we consider them exclusively from the viewpoint of the readers' advisor. We briefly touch on signs, book displays, bookmarks, booktalks, and the layout of the readers' advisory area. Basic how-to information on these topics can be found in the current library literature, and we have no intention of duplicating this.

We have also included a more detailed section on how to produce annotated book lists. Since we have found little information available about the basics involved in their creation, and even less that applies to the type of book lists we recommend for readers' advisory work, we have developed our own techniques.

First Impressions

Often, unfortunately, an individual librarian can do little about the physical arrangement of the library. Decisions such as where the librarian's service desk is located, how the books are arranged, and what signs are being used are often made by others or cannot be altered. To the extent possible, however, readers' advisors should make sure that the library's layout and design call attention to their activities and encourage both patron contact and easy book selection. As we have said before, readers' advisors cannot expect that patrons will necessarily seek them out; thus, the location of the service desk should be thoughtfully chosen to draw the notice of readers. Ideally, readers' advisors should situate themselves as close to the fiction collection, especially to the new books, as is convenient, because these are often a reader's first stop. Readers' advisors not only need to be visible; they also need space at their service area for reference materials, book lists, and bookmarks, as well as access to the book collection either by card catalog or by computer.

Consider and pursue any options that make the library as comfortable as possible for readers as they look at books and talk with readers' advisors. For example, shelving that displays book covers forward, seats that allow better vision of low shelving, and good lighting are the kinds of details that encourage browsing and facilitate conversations about books. Comfortable seating in the fiction area also helps create an atmosphere that underlines the importance of reading and is conducive to leisurely book selection. Simple adjustments will often come to mind if we take a good look at the library from the reader's point of view. Since studies have shown that a high proportion of fiction readers are browsers, everything we can do to make browsing and selecting easier will benefit our collection and its users.[1]

Clear and readable signs should advertise and promote the readers' advisory service. Signs such as "Ask Here for a Good Book," or "Not Sure What to Read? Ask Here," or even the simple "Readers' Advisory Service" all alert readers. We post *Rosenberg's First Law of Reading: Never apologize for your reading tastes* behind our service desk because it reinforces our philosophy about suggesting books and encourages patrons to approach us to discuss books. The sign has often been commented on by patrons and has provided the impetus for many very satisfying readers' advisory interviews.

Providing good, clear signs and an inviting and efficient physical arrangement is the first step in creating an atmosphere conducive to readers' advisory activities. Time spent looking at possible options will be repaid in increased visibility and a more accessible readers' advisory service.

Segregated Genre Collections

In chapter 1, we mentioned that the arrangement of the fiction collection—alphabetically by author—creates problems for browsing readers and argues in favor of providing readers' advisory to assist readers find books they will enjoy. Grouping the fiction collection by genre and/or placing genre identification on book spines is often suggested as the solution to providing readers with better access to the collection. We readers' advisors know how frequently readers request materials by genre, and increased research in the past years supports the effectiveness of genre fiction categorization.[2] In addition, a recent study indicates the popularity of genre categories in libraries serving larger populations, with "Science Fiction and/or Fantasy," "Westerns," and "Detective and/or Mystery and/or Suspense" used in more than ninety percent of the libraries surveyed.[3] More than eighty percent of those libraries also shelve these collections separately.[4]

While we advocate, and indeed practice, some genre fiction classification and collection segregation at the Downers Grove Public Library, we do not believe that classification alone is the answer. One problem is that genre labeling and/or classification is not a straightforward task. As anyone who has tried to classify fiction realizes, it is difficult to label novels or authors by genre with any integrity or consistency. There is also the danger that classification will segregate readers, allowing them to believe that if they like Mysteries, for example, they will find books they will enjoy only in that area. Classification and separation by genre may also reinforce the misconception that fiction selection should be done without bothering the library staff. In addition, genre classification alone does not help readers find the particular types of authors or titles they are looking for *within* a genre. As anyone who has worked with readers knows, locating books within a genre is only the first step for genre fans in selecting reading material. Readers' advisors provide assistance in locating the type of book a particular reader might enjoy, suggesting from among the numerous genres, subgenres, and appeals.

While both can help, neither a classification system nor increased subject access can truly serve the readers' advisory function. Facilitating optimum use of the fiction collection and serving individual readers well require trained staff, whether or not fiction is classified by genre. A parallel can be drawn between readers' advisory service and library service to users of nonfiction material. Although subject classification, subject headings, and print guides such as pathfinders can be helpful to nonfiction users, these reference tools are not expected to do the whole job. The full potential of information and reference material is realized only when patrons have expert reference librarians available to assist them. These same standards and philosophy should be applied to the service provided to users of the fiction collection. While some level of genre classification and segregation can help readers and readers' advisors alike, we need to be careful in choosing which genres we segregate, selecting those in which fairly clear distinctions, easily understood by all users of the collection, can be made.

Book Exhibits

A book exhibit consisting of a small group of books and a descriptive sign is one of the most effective ways to promote and highlight parts of the fiction collection. In this section, we discuss a more or less permanent display we use, as well as short-term displays.

An ongoing Good Books You May Have Missed exhibit has, in fact, been one of the most useful book promotion ideas we have ever had. On a metal book truck near the readers' advisory desk, which is at the entrance to the fiction section, we keep a small, selected group of books. Instead of trying to find a "good read" from the rather daunting numbers of books available in the book stacks, here patrons have a small group of suggested titles from which to choose.

The Good Books You May Have Missed cart has up to twenty-one books spread out on the three shelves of a one-sided library book truck. A large sign above the cart proclaims Good Books You May Have Missed. Books are displayed with covers out, alternating with books displayed with spines out. The Good Books You May Have Missed truck is monitored by readers' advisory staff during their scheduled time at the desk. If some of the titles have been removed by patrons, the books remaining on the book truck are first rearranged so that titles that were spine out are now cover out and vice versa. The books are also moved upward, leaving all empty spots on the bottom shelves. In order to maintain the twenty-one-book maximum, staff add new books to the bottom shelves. One day a week, a staff member notes what is on the top shelf. Any books that remain on the book truck after a week are removed and new titles added, again always moving the remaining books upward and adding new titles at the bottom. This simple system gives every book an equal chance at exposure and ensures that the collection is always fresh. We keep track of the number of books we add to the truck and cumulate the figures monthly, comparing figures over time.

Books to be placed in the Good Books You May Have Missed display are those with our longest checkout period, i.e., our older books. We include primarily hardcover books with book jackets because they are the most attractive and eye-catching. We choose mass-market paperbacks less frequently, as we find that most of them are too small to display well. The titles we put on the book truck are some of the best examples of the different genres. An effort is made to include quality popular fiction as well as old favorites. We also strive to have a variety of genres on display, making sure that the most popular genres in our library are represented.

Patron response to this ongoing exhibit has been gratifying, to say the least. On rare occasions, we have had to discontinue the display for a short time, and at those times there has always been a great deal of consternation among the patrons who visit the display regularly. Patrons often tell us that it is their first or last stop when they come to the library.

There are a number of advantages to the Good Books You May Have Missed exhibit. It is easy to maintain, and it places the better, older fiction before the public. Because the Good Books You May Have Missed truck is filled by whoever is at the readers' advisory desk, we all have an opportunity to refresh our memories of titles we might suggest to readers. This system also guarantees a wider variety of titles than if only one person always makes the selections. Since we make an effort to select good books and try to maintain a variety of genres, the act of deciding which books to add to the display heightens our awareness of the quality and the genre classification of various titles. In addition, watching which types of books are circulating and which are not gives us an informal assessment of what is popular at any given time. The exhibit is also a form of readers' advisory fail-safe. Here is a preselected group of books we draw upon when our minds have gone blank or when we want to ascertain a reader's tastes by describing several genres or types of books, for we are likely to find a representative selection on the book truck.

Our Good Books You May Have Missed book truck is an ongoing exhibit, but thematic book exhibits of shorter duration are another way we showcase the fiction collection. We find that for readers' advisory work, the most effective displays are ones from which readers can select books and immediately check them out, not the locked-cabinet type. If the displays are movable (for example, books on a single-sided book truck), they become even more flexible.

We also have found that displays of twenty to thirty books are about the right size. A display showing only three or four books on exhibit looks uninviting, and too many books can be overwhelming. The key is to make sure, before we put up the book exhibit, that enough good titles are available beyond the first twenty so that the exhibit can be properly stocked for the expected time it will run. A display for which we have only twenty or so possible titles will have a short life and will rapidly look fairly bedraggled since patrons will check out most of the titles, and we will not be able to restock the display. Occasionally we will do weeklong, rather than monthlong, displays of books on a subject for which there may be a great deal of interest but not enough titles to support a longer display.

In our experience, good displays capitalize on the elements of books that appeal to readers. For example, we have put fast-paced Espionage Thrillers under the sign "If You Like Robert Ludlum's Thrillers, Try One of These." We also use displays that take advantage of readers' moods. For instance, in the dead of winter, we used a collection of Family Sagas and Storyteller novels under the sign "Books for a Long Winter Night." Subject exhibits are still another type—sea stories or books with foreign settings, for example. We also display staff-produced bookmarks and book lists, along with appropriate titles. We choose themes that reflect what we feel our readers would enjoy reading. Like the books in the Good Books You May Have Missed display, the selected titles are ones that have been read by someone in the department or that are suggested by a reliable source, such as *Fiction Catalog*. We do not display just any book that happens to fall within the theme; we try to be more discriminating. Readers grow to trust the quality of the books we put on display, so we make a point of selecting them carefully.

In contrast, an example of an exhibit that may be fun but that does not promote readers' advisory service is the Books That Have Never Been Checked Out type. Unless the book selection for this kind of display is very carefully done—focusing on good material that will truly appeal to readers—the display will be of limited value to both readers and readers' advisors. Perhaps there is a good reason why the titles have not circulated.

In dividing up the total time set aside for creating book displays, we spend the majority of time choosing a theme that will appeal to readers and selecting titles to include. The smaller percentage of time is spent creating the display itself. Because of the time and care taken with book selection, these displays become a reliable source of titles for readers and readers' advisors alike. Signs advertising the display need not be elaborate; the simpler the better is the rule we try to follow. Since the purpose of the display is to put books in readers' hands, we try to make it attractive and inviting without it appearing to be part of a do-not-touch exhibit. We find that a clear, basic setup and good titles are what bring readers back. Librarians fortunate enough to have talented artists with time to devote to creating more elaborate displays can build on this basic display format. On the other hand, it should be reassuring to librarians who lack budget, staff, and/or skills to devise more decorative displays that basic displays can be just as successful and popular among readers.

An additional, related promotional idea that we have found to be very effective is an ongoing, and regularly changing, display of the bookmarks and annotated book lists our department has produced over the years. We all know that many patrons like to browse on their own, and they are pleased to find a selection of book lists on a wide range of topics; they can choose one or more and simply take them into the stacks with them as a guide to reading suggestions. This is another low-maintenance display. We have a file cabinet of bookmarks and book lists, and a clerk changes half the display every week. Our library has a display unit that holds a mix of approximately sixteen bookmarks and annotated book lists, but even a spot to put out copies of lists at the service desk, at the circulation disk, or in a unit that attaches to the end of a book stack would inexpensively serve the same purpose.

We have designated places for both ongoing and short-term book displays. One of the benefits of an established display area is that patrons know where to go to find a changing and interesting selection of books, and this feature affects their perception of the library's attitude toward reading and books.

Bookmarks

Bookmarks are another method we use to highlight parts of the fiction collection. A bookmark, as you might expect, is more complicated and time-consuming to produce than a display. The advantage of a bookmark, however, is that the reader can walk away not only with a book to read but also with a list of authors and titles to pursue on a later visit. Each of our bookmarks consists of a list of authors and titles. They are printed on sturdy card stock so that they will stand up in a display unit. They usually are not annotated. Of course, even a one-line comment about each title makes a bookmark more valuable to the user, but producing such a description increases the work load for the bookmark's creator.

We have found that the most useful bookmarks focus on limited subject areas for which full annotations are not necessary. Examples of bookmarks with a narrow enough focus are Locked-Room Mysteries and If You Like [*Author Name*], Try These. When produced, the bookmark is made available for patrons, along with a display of the listed books. We have found that we need to be exceedingly careful in our bookmark subject selection because not every topic lends itself to this format. The subjects of bookmarks need to be straightforward and self-explanatory. Whenever the reader will need more information in order to make a choice among the titles, it is better to undertake an annotated book list. And just a reminder: Any and all printed materials need extensive proofreading. We will discuss proofreading in more detail in the next section, Annotated Book Lists.

Bookmarks have several advantages. They require much less work than an annotated book list, but at the same time they give readers a selected list of authors and titles that are available in the library. Bookmarks can be compiled to aid readers' advisory staff in meeting the need for books on popular topics, such as novels featuring lawyers or Techno-Thrillers. Creating a bookmark also exposes a novice bibliographer to the process of choosing a theme and selecting books related to patrons' interests and to the rigors of proofreading, which can be substantial, as is made obvious in the next section, Annotated Book Lists. As well as having their own place in the promotion of reading, bookmarks are a good first step for someone who wants to create annotated book lists. There is, in fact, a progression with respect to the skills and time required from designing displays, to compiling bookmarks, to creating book lists.

Another, more specific and difficult, bookmark links similar authors under a title like, "If you enjoy the Suspense novels of Mary Higgins Clark, try one of these." The bookmarks of choice for many of our patrons, these are the bane of our existence because they are so hard to compile. What we are *not* creating is a list of one hundred diverse Horror writers and claiming they write "just like" Stephen King. Readers are more discriminating than that, and we need to be, too. Unfortunately, we have yet to find a reference source—book or electronic—that produces a reliable list.

The problem seems to be that these lists truly draw more on appeal than subject, and reference sources do not address this more nebulous factor. We do use these commercial resources as a place to start, to brainstorm possible authors to include, and we let patrons react—positively and negatively—to these suggestions.

Having said this, we must add that our lists, despite the fact that we understand how they have to be constructed and that we spend hours considering these links, are not perfect either. We do feel confident that they reflect the *range* of an author's appeal. We know from experience that authors appeal to different readers for a variety of reasons. For example, some readers like Larry McMurtry for his western settings and landscape details, and they enjoy a range of books with similar settings. Others read him for his elegant writing style and depth of characterization. No list of similar authors is perfect for every reader.

This type of bookmark usually grows out of our need to supply a particular author's fans with more books they will enjoy. In chapter 5, we suggested that creating such a list can be both the impetus to embarking on a genre study and the end product of such a study. When we decide to create such a list, we brainstorm the appeal characteristics of this popular author and note them on a piece of paper taped to our service desk. Then readers' advisory staff list other authors who might fill the need. We list the authors and then try them out with readers. If they agree that these seem "just like," the authors go on our list. Every name and title that ultimately appear on the list have been tested—by us and other readers. Clearly, compiling these lists requires a certain level of expertise and a knowledge of fiction, appeal, and readers, not to mention extensive reading of possible titles, both those that do ultimately appear on the list and those that prove not to be appropriate.

Annotated Book Lists

Because locally produced annotated book lists provide readers with a printed list of suggested books available in the library, they are an important tool for readers' advisory work. Despite this fact, not much has been written about them from a readers' advisory point of view. For this reason, we believe that it is important to consider book lists—their construction and their value—in some detail.

It is worth noting at the outset that producing original

annotated book lists takes time. The bibliographer must choose a topic, select appropriate books, write annotations, prepare copy for printing, and set up the display of books with the finished book list. Although we have worked to streamline these activities, we have found that each requires considerable time and effort. We believe, however, that the advantages of locally produced annotated book lists make the effort an extremely valuable exercise and worthwhile to the creator, the staff, and the patrons.

Producing an annotated book list on a topic extends the creator's knowledge of the topic and of the range of books that fall within it. Bibliographers narrow or expand a topic to suit the scope they define, and they read and read about books within that topic. Then they crystallize their impressions of the chosen books into inviting annotations. Again, this is no small task, but it is not one without rewards.

For patrons, annotated book lists furnish booklets that include not just book titles, but descriptions as well. Readers go away with a list—something tangible in addition to any books they select. In fact, there is nothing more satisfying than coming upon a patron in the stacks, clutching a dog-eared book list and choosing from among the books included on it. Annotated book lists provide some of the benefits of readers' advisory to patrons who feel uncomfortable talking with staff about their reading interests.

Before we discuss the process of creating book lists, we want to elaborate on two points: Book lists for fiction need to be annotated, and they should reflect the local library's collection. First, working primarily with fiction as we do, we have strong feelings about the necessity of creating *annotated* book lists and believe that, although the time required may be the same, our time is far better spent producing one annotated book list than four unannotated ones. One reason for annotating fiction book lists is obvious: It is often impossible to tell anything about a work of fiction just from its title. Annotations are necessary to describe the book. Second, although it is possible to reap some benefits from commercially produced book lists, we feel that the real advantage to readers' advisors and patrons alike comes from locally produced book lists, which include books from the library's collection on topics based on the staff's perceptions of reader interests.

The procedure we follow in creating our book lists is explained below. It concentrates primarily on how readers' advisors think through both the theme and content of a book list, and it offers some guidelines for proofreading and display. The process falls into five stages: choosing a topic, selecting books and defining the scope of the book list, writing the annotations, preparing the book list for printing, and displaying the completed book list.

Choosing the Topic and
Defining the Scope

Choosing a topic that reflects reader interests is our first step in producing an annotated book list. Sometimes an appropriate topic comes easily to mind, as when, for example, there have been a number of requests for books with western themes or for a more complex topic, such as page-turners, for which authors cannot easily be found in either book or electronic reference sources. When we are having difficulty choosing a topic, we check our log of patron comments and questions. A number of requests for a genre such as Horror or for a specific writer such as Stephen King may mean that Horror would be a good candidate for an annotated book list. We might read through subject headings in *Fiction Catalog* or browse through a collection of book lists from other libraries, as these activities often remind us of a topic that would interest patrons and make a good book list. Brainstorming ideas among the readers' advisory staff has also proved useful when we are at a loss for a topic. In fact, at least once a year we have a session to generate ideas for future book lists. Staff members can often identify appropriate subjects by talking through requests they have found difficult to fill.

Although we need to choose a topic that reflects the needs and interests of our patrons, we also have to be certain the bibliographer is comfortable with and enthusiastic about the chosen topic. After all, since the staff member will likely be reading and annotating almost two dozen books, the topic must reflect the readers' advisor's interest as well. There have been times when we have needed a book list on a topic about which no one was enthusiastic. Then, rather than assigning it to someone or even taking it on personally, we decided to do a department book list, with everyone contributing just a few annotations. Not only were the discussion and title negotiations interesting and useful, but the finished book list was far superior to anything we could have written individually.

Once a topic has been chosen, the next step is to collect a large number and variety of books for the book list. As the readers' advisor begins making decisions about which to include, questions arise; in answering these questions and in considering the purpose of the book list, the advisor defines its scope. This task requires the staff member to decide what to focus on within the topic and to determine the audience for the list. For example, with a book list highlighting new books on a subject, the readers' advisor quickly sees that in order to select books, an appropriate cutoff date is needed, and only new books published after that date should be included. When a book list of foreign fiction was compiled in our library, for instance, the advisor was forced to consider whether to include only native authors whose works had been translated into English or books by non-natives with foreign settings. In the case of the proposed book list of Family Sagas, terms had to be defined. For example, what constitutes a Family Saga? Is it about two generations of a family? Three? What makes a book a Family Saga and not a family story, a Historical Novel, or simply part of a series?

In defining the scope of the topic, readers' advisors should also ask who the intended audience is. Is a genre book list compiled for fans who have read within the genre or for nonfans in order to provide an overview or an introduction? Is the book list directed at a particular age group, such as young adults? Or is the subject something like Small Town Life, which, with a mix of books ranging from Romance and Gentle Read to Mystery and Horror, is designed to appeal to a wide variety of readers? Considering the audience for whom the book list is designed and evaluating titles from that point of view help readers' advisors define the book list's scope and make decisions about which titles should ultimately be included.

We have found that it is always useful to put the topic and scope into words as early as possible in the process, defining what ties the books together. We will occasionally discover that the proposed scope is too narrow, that there are not enough acceptable and appropriate titles available, and we must rethink and expand the scope. In fact, this statement explaining the scope is often included at the beginning of a printed book list, because it sets the stage for the books and annotations that follow. As an example, the following scope statement for an annotated book list entitled "Novels with a Touch of Science" reflects the nature of the books included:

> To read a book that explores science in a painless manner, try one of these books that teaches an aspect of the natural sciences or the scientific method using a fictional setting. The books range in topic from physics to paleontology to geology and beyond.[5]

Selecting the Books

Once we have a clear definition of the book list's scope and an idea of the list's intended audience, we make final decisions about which books to include. The titles chosen for a book list must fit the scope, but they must also meet certain standards. Books included in a book list must be *known* to be books of an acceptable quality, either because we have read them ourselves or because they are listed in a trustworthy source to which we can refer if questions of suitability ever arise. Annotated book lists allow us, as readers' advisors, to put our book suggestions into print for patrons. Thus, we want to be careful in our selection of titles.

How many books should be included? We generally annotate eighteen to twenty-four titles, primarily because that number fits comfortably on a folded legal-size sheet of paper, the size we most frequently use. We feel that fewer titles provide too small a sample for the user and make the process hardly worth the effort for the readers' advisor. More titles make the book list cumbersome to produce, as additional pages are required and more time is needed to write the annotations. We do, however, make certain that more than just the eighteen to twenty-four listed titles on this theme are in our fiction collection, since we always display the book list with books, both those we have annotated and other appropriate titles.

Our selection guidelines include three additional caveats. First, we include no more than one book by an author. If readers like the title by that author, they will read others. One well-chosen title is enough to get readers started, and limiting the book list to one title per author allows us to include more authors. The exception is if an author writes different types of books and more than one type fits the scope of the book list. Second, we seldom include original mass-market paperbacks on annotated book lists. Our concern is simply that paperbacks, because they are inexpensively produced with cheaper paper and binding, often have short lives. When we consider the time and effort involved in producing book lists, we prefer to focus on books that will likely remain in our collection longer. We expect to keep and use book lists for several years, and paperback originals, especially, are often out of print and unavailable sooner than we plan to update or discard the book list. Third, we try to include as wide a variety of titles as fit within the defined scope. For example, a book list of fiction set during World War II produced by one staff member covered not only stories of battles but also life away from the Front in England

and America, Espionage Novels, and Suspense Stories. Thus, it appealed to a larger audience than it would have had it concentrated only on battle stories.

Writing Annotations

After the topic has been selected, the scope defined, and appropriate books chosen, the bibliographer is ready to begin writing the annotations.

> To shun the hackneyed phrase, the threadbare adjective, to find the word that conveys the nature of the book's style or distills the essence of its theme, to integrate its substance, quality, and value clearly, logically, and with graphic brevity, is to practice the fine art of annotation.[6]

Thus wrote Helen E. Haines in 1950, defining the art of annotation writing—another art to which readers' advisors aspire, and one closely related to the technique of describing books orally. Just as some readers' advisors have the facility to talk easily about books with readers, others can do the same in writing: They can capture the essence of a book in a sentence or two and make you want to pull the book off the shelf and read it immediately. Most of us must work to perfect these skills.

Good annotations should be both informative and inviting; they should describe a book in a way that makes readers want to read it and yet give enough plot information to allow readers to judge if this is the book for them. Annotations for fiction book lists should focus on the story line and on the book's appeal to the reader. The text of the annotation should leave no doubt about the kind of book being described. The annotation should show how the book fits within the scope of the book list, and it should focus on the book's best feature, just as readers' advisors do in their conversations with readers. The key is to write an inviting annotation without overpraising the book—and without giving the ending away.

Regarding style, the best annotations are written in the active rather than the passive voice. We have found that, while annotations need not be grammatically complete sentences, they must flow. It is not necessary to use a subject if the subject would be the book's title or the words "this book"; in fact, there is no point to repeating the title or information implied by the title in the annotation itself. Also, reading the annotation aloud is a technique that sometimes helps determine if it will be readily understood. Finally, annotations should be concise, preferably just one or two sentences long and fewer than one hundred words. We have learned that each bibliographer has a different style of writing annotations; while we do not intend the above guidelines to stifle creativity, we have found them helpful in structuring the annotation.

We have all experienced those difficult times when we simply cannot seem to write *anything*, not to mention something as difficult as good annotations. We have found that the best way to get around this block is to think about each of the books with respect to the scope of the book list: What is it about the book that makes it fit? Why would the person who picks up the book list want to read that particular book? Thinking in these terms often gets us writing again.

One difficulty we have discovered in attempting to write inviting annotations is that there are very few good models to follow. Among our peers, we librarians often discuss books in critical terms. Book reviews are designed to do the same—to be critical of the book, to point out faults as well as strengths in order to help a librarian decide whether to purchase a particular title. Thus, the reviews we spend so much time reading are poor models for readers' advisory work in general and annotation writing in particular. Annotations for book lists focus on the parts of the book that appeal to readers. Annotators select and promote good books; they do not need to evaluate them critically as well. For more tips on writing annotations, consult Mary K. Chelton's "Read Any Good Books Lately? Helping Patrons Find What They Want," where she discusses "How to Write a Reader's Annotation," and Sharon L. Baker's "Book Lists: What We Know, What We Need to Know."[7] Although we agree on some points, our styles and opinions often differ, thus giving prospective annotation writers varying points of view to draw from in developing their own styles.

While there are some similarities between annotations for book lists and those for annotation cards (see chapter 5), they differ in focus and purpose. The annotation card has a uniform format that requires the same information about all titles (setting, subject headings, etc.) and a more extensive plot summary based on the range of the book's appeal to the reader. Book list annotations, on the other hand, briefly highlight one or more aspects of appeal and focus on how the book fits in with the scope of the book list. For example, if a readers' advisor were to use Jane Langton's *Dead as a Dodo* for that annotated book list of "Novels with a Touch of Science," mentioned above, the annotator might high-light the discussion of Darwin and his evolutionary theory, which permeates the text, and the fact that Langton uses appropriately chosen passages from Darwin's writing to head many chapters.[8] A book list on mysteries in a college or university setting would cer-tainly place greater emphasis on the Oxford setting—especially the Museum of Oxford—the cadence of university life and interactions between professors and students, perhaps the additional quotations from Lewis Carroll that balance the more serious lines from Darwin, and Langton's multiple drawings, which evoke the Oxford scene. The annotation card would touch on all these aspects of appeal and subject interests. Clearly, book list annotations are shorter and more focused than annotation sheet plot summaries and reflect the more limited scope of the book list.

We are still grappling with another issue involved in writing annotations for book lists: What is and is not copyrighted? As with many issues related to copyright law, absolutely clear guidelines are not provided. Haines wrote in 1950,

> In the preparation of such lists, annotations in current and standard bibliographical guides as well as terse comments from reviews or graphic summations from publishers' announce-ments are drawn upon for information, for adaptation or para-phrase.[9]

The issue is, of course, when is it paraphrase and not quotation?

What about the book description on book jackets? Are they copyrighted or "fair game"? When asked, legal experts replied that the material on a book jacket is exempt from copyright law if the information being quoted is factual information about the book or an outline of factual information. This information is considered advertising for the book. If the information to be quoted is a fairly elaborate synopsis of the plot, it is protected by law. Again, the issue is not straightforward, but it seems likely that anything beyond the basics, any character or plot description, would be protected.

Although we do not have any clear-cut answers on the copy-right issue, we believe that readers' advisors need to be conscious of and sensitive to this issue. Certainly, one cannot copy annotations from another source and not credit the source. However, there is obviously a very fine line between copying and Haines's concept of "adaptation or paraphrase." We advise reading the book or about the book and writing annotations from our impressions of every-thing we have read. If we take something word for word from another source, we put the material in quotations and credit our source. The rights of the original authors to their own words must be respected, and we feel that it behooves all librarians to be aware of the dangers of simply copying someone else's words.

This discussion brings up another issue that arises whenever book lists are considered: Do we need to read every book we include? We do not believe that it is necessary to read every book; however, we do believe that we must be doubly certain that the books we have not read are of the desired quality and that they fit within the scope of the topic we have chosen. As we all know, book reviews and book jackets do not always give a complete and accurate picture of a book, so we are careful not to rely on them exclusively. When considering a book we have not read, we talk to people who have read the book, check several reviews and other descriptions of the book, and skim the book judiciously. Most staff consider simply reading the book easier and more efficient.

All these issues—from style to content—need to be considered in writing annotations for book lists. In the end, we believe that the secret to writing inviting annotations is enthusiasm for the book, just as it is the key to talking about books with readers. Some readers' advisors can write inviting annotations but have difficulty talking with readers about those same books. Others can "sell" almost any book verbally but have trouble doing the same in print. The art of annotation writing is the ability to capture a reader's enthusiasm for a book, to think about the best elements of the book, and to convey each of these aspects in writing to other readers.

Preparing to Print

Choosing a topic, defining its scope and selecting books to include, and writing annotations make up the first three stages in compiling an annotated book list. At the fourth stage, the book list is prepared for printing, which involves setting up the final format, editing, and proofreading.

First, a few words about format. In our annotations, we include the following bibliographic information: author, title, publication date, and number of pages, as well as the call number or location in our collection. The reasons for these inclusions are covered in our discussion of annotation sheets in chapter 5. Our policy is to put the name of the bibliographer, the date the book list was produced, a request not to copy without permission, and the library logo with library name, address, and telephone number at the end of our book lists. What a library can do regarding the physical format of its book lists often depends on the resources available and the amount of money it chooses to put into the production of such materials. We have found that colored legal-size paper folded in half to make four nearly square pages is a convenient and workable size. We devote the top three to four inches of the first page to the title and to any graphics, and then we simply run the annotations—usually in alphabetical order by author. This format requires a minimum of time, effort, and money, and it produces a simple but attractive book list.

Editing is the next aspect in this process. We designate one person as editor for each book list. It need not be the same person every time, but it is important to have someone fill this role from the book list's beginning. In the early stages, the editor is a sounding board for ideas—someone to provide assistance in defining the scope, selecting books, and writing annotations. The editor asks several questions at this stage: Is there a good mix of book types? Is there as much variety as possible within the scope of the topic? Are there too many examples of one kind of book? The editor works with the creator in striving for a balance among all the possible types of books that could be included.

The editor reads for style and content, as well as for grammatical errors: Is the style of the annotations consistent without being monotonous? Are the annotations approximately the same length? There is certainly some room for variation in the length of the annotations, but if some are quite long and others quite short, there may be a problem that needs to be addressed. Is there a legitimate reason for the variation? Do the shorter annotations say enough? Are the longer ones simply wordy? Do the annotations adequately describe the story line? Simply saying that the book is "a good read" is not sufficient; the bibliographer needs to provide evidence to convince readers of this fact. Are the annotations inviting? Do they describe the story in a way that will intrigue the reader? In our experience, the last sentence of the annotation is often crucial and should be constructed with care to be especially interesting and hook the reader. Finally, are there jarring remarks or language in the annotations? The editor should read carefully and check that the annotations are nonprejudicial and noncritical. If there are any reservations about a book, that book should not be included on the list.

Proofreading is the final step in creating a book list. We place a lot of emphasis on this step because we have *never* had a book list in which the proofreader has not found errors, no matter how careful the creator and editor were. Proofreading should be done after all editorial changes have been made and the book list is essentially ready for printing. The first rule of proofreading is that this task must be done by someone who has never seen the book list before; therefore, both the creator and the editor are excluded from this process. You may need to enlist colleagues or others outside the library to help. The easiest method we have found is to collect all the books included in the book list and have the proofreader sit down with the books and the book lists and verify the information using the proofreading checklist (see Figure 6.1).

We do not mention checking for spelling errors as being among either the editor's or the proofreader's responsibilities; however, both individuals must look for misspelled words. For the most part, finding spelling errors hinges on whether a word looks questionable to the reader. Both the editor and the proofreader must take responsibility for checking for spelling errors and look up

Figure 6.1
Downers Grove Public Library Proofreading Checklist

Check each annotation for the following:

1. Alphabetization or organization of entries.
2. Author's full name—exactly as it appears on the title page.
3. All title words and punctuation in the title—exactly as they appear on the title page.
4. Publication/copyright date.
5. Number of pages.
6. Call number or location information.
7. Any personal and place names used in the annotation.

Check also for:

1. Name of bibliographer.
2. Library logo, address, and telephone number.
3. Date.

any questionable words. We type our book lists on a word processor and use a spelling checker. However, we do not rely on the spelling checker exclusively because it will not catch mistakes such as homonyms if the inappropriate word has been correctly spelled.

Now for some final cautions. In general, we advise our staff never to include anything in a book list or annotation that they are not willing or able to check. We also want to stress again that no matter how accurate you are, *you cannot proofread your own work.* Doing this is possible theoretically—if you are willing and able to read the book list backwards, word by word—but it is hardly advisable if it can be avoided. It is better to find good proofreaders among your staff and friends and to employ their skills. Our experience is that good proofreaders generally enjoy the task and are willing to help. Furthermore, if you make changes in the original, the altered entries need to be checked again after the corrections have been made. Proofreading takes time—always more than expected. However, the assurance it gives that you are providing accurate material for publication makes proofreading necessary and worthwhile.

Displaying the Book List

Displaying the book list is the final stage of the production process. We exhibit all newly produced book lists alongside the listed books and other appropriate titles. We feel that it is important to display the book lists with the books, even if we simply put both on a book truck at the end of a book stack. The completed list can then be included in the display of our older book lists in a freestanding display unit. As mentioned earlier, patrons often browse through these lists when they are looking for book suggestions; readers' advisors, in talking with readers, can also refer to book lists on the display and easily give them to patrons as part of the readers' advisory interview.

We believe that it is important for a library that wants to provide annotated book lists to produce its own lists, featuring books from its collection and focusing on subjects of particular interest to its readers. However, we do not believe this to be an activity limited strictly to professional librarians. Book lists of the type we describe can be created by anyone who is willing to make the commitment in time and effort. The key is enthusiasm for books and for the subject.

Booktalks

Booktalking is an art, and when done well, it can be entertaining as well as informative for the audience. Several books and articles have been written about how to booktalk.[10] If booktalking is an activity you are unfamiliar with, a survey of the literature, especially in the young adult and children's areas, should provide you with several informative sources. Our purpose in adding a section on booktalks, as in several other sections in this chapter, is not to discuss the basic techniques but to suggest an approach that we feel complements the philosophy and general goals of readers' advisory service.

We had been looking for a way to use booktalks to reflect the work we were already doing as readers' advisors. When we came upon the answer, it at first seemed so simple that it took us awhile to appreciate its advantages: We began to apply the same guidelines to booktalking that we use in our readers' advisory interviews and in other promotional activities. When gathering the titles, we do not limit our choices only to books we personally have read. We think instead about the types of books that might appeal to the audience; thus, the more we know about the group we are to address, the better we can focus our selections. We plan to spend about five minutes presenting each book, although we are fairly flexible from book to book. When describing each title, we use the techniques outlined in the section of chapter 4 called Talking about Books. We emphasize the elements that make the book appeal to a reader; we describe the best features of the book, perhaps even reading a passage to help emphasize a point; and then we make comparisons to well-known authors and titles, or even to other books by that same author, including remarks such as, "If you are the kind of reader who enjoys [*popular author's name*], you may enjoy this book, too." We also make it clear to the audience that one of our jobs as readers' advisors is to suggest books and to evaluate titles in terms of how they appeal to readers; they should come ask us whenever they want reading suggestions.

Again, some staff are naturals at talking before a group—they make books and reading them sound irresistible. Still, by using the skills of describing and selecting titles already practiced in conducting readers' advisory interviews, *all* readers' advisors can attempt this type of booktalk. The booktalks we are recommending directly support the readers' advisory service because they introduce the audience to the type of book suggesting that readers' advisors regularly do. Developing booktalks can also expand the skills of readers' advisors in describing titles, encouraging readers' advisors again to focus on a book's appeal and on readers' tastes.

We have found that all of the activities discussed in this chapter have a place in readers' advisory service. The value of these promotional suggestions as readers' advisory tools is that they rely on and support basic readers' advisory techniques and acknowledge the reader's perspective with respect to the layout of the department, displays, printed bookmarks, book lists, and booktalks. In the next chapter, Training, we look at a readers' advisory training program, a way to support the initial and continuing education of a readers' advisory staff.

Notes

1. Sharon L. Baker, "A Decade Worth of Research on Browsing Fiction Collections," in *Guiding the Reader to the Next Book,* 127–47.
2. Ibid., 141–47.
3. Gail Harrel, "Use of Fiction Categories in Major American Public Libraries," in *Guiding the Reader to the Next Book,* 150.
4. Ibid., 151.
5. Sue O'Brien, "Novels with a Touch of Science" (Downers Grove Public Library, Downers Grove, Ill., annotated book list, April 1992).
6. Helen E. Haines, *Living with Books: The Art of Book Selection* (New York: Columbia Univ. Pr., 1950), 145.
7. Mary K. Chelton, "Read Any Good Books Lately? Helping Patrons Find What They Want," *Library Journal* 118 (May 1993): 33–37; and Sharon L. Baker, "Book Lists: What We Know, What We Need to Know," *RQ* 33 (Winter 1993): 177–80.
8. Jane Langton, *Dead as a Dodo* (New York: Viking, 1996).
9. Haines, 140.
10. Mary K. Shelton, "Booktalking: You Can Do It," *School Library Journal* 22 (April 1976): 39–44; Joni Bodart, *Booktalk!* (Bronx, N.Y.: Wilson, 1980); and Hazel Rochman, *Tales of Love and Terror: Booktalking the Classics, Old and New* (Chicago: American Library Assn., 1987).

7 Training

Training staff in the art of readers' advisory is, in many ways, the most difficult task we undertake. Training requires energy, inspiration, animation, and enthusiasm, as well as the ability to work at the top of our form as we model correct behavior. Providing ongoing training that is designed to keep staff enthusiastic, up-to-date, and growing as readers' advisors is as challenging and time-consuming as instilling philosophy and skills in new staff.

The focus of this chapter will be on *what,* not *how,* to train, and it will draw on information presented in more detail in the previous chapters. All of us have our own styles and timetables. How we implement readers' advisory service and train staff to provide this service is not the essential issue; what we train and that this training provides a sound basis for skill development are critical.

Very few librarians required to provide readers' advisory service have had formal library school training in public service techniques useful in dealing with patrons or any background in popular fiction, the primary collection used in providing this service. In probably no other aspect of library work is on-the-job (and even less formal) training more often the rule rather than the exception. Only in recent years are library schools beginning to offer such training, acknowledging that preparing graduates in this area is absolutely crucial in enabling them to work successfully with adults in public libraries. Many individual public libraries and library systems, on the other hand, have instigated extensive and elaborate continuing

Figure 7.1
Goals of Readers' Advisory Training

1. Help staff (and the administration) recognize the importance of and the need to provide readers' advisory service in the library.

2. Teach readers' advisors to be comfortable, skilled, and nonjudgmental in their interactions with readers.

3. Provide strategies so readers' advisors can be successful in going from readers' interests, moods, and needs to books as they suggest a range of possible titles patrons might wish to read.

4. Help readers' advisors understand the concept of appeal and its essential role in readers' advisory work.

---

education programs that focus on readers' advisory training. Some libraries provide genre overviews or offer formal instruction to increase staff knowledge of popular genres, in addition to teaching basic readers' advisory techniques. Other libraries have implemented directed reading programs and assign readers' advisory reference questions as training exercises. Whatever we do, we need to help staff gain familiarity with readers' advisory techniques and popular fiction genres through reading, practice, and discussion.

This chapter will highlight those areas in which training is vital, providing both an intellectual and a philosophical justification for such training, and will present specific activities that help staff build skills. First, however, it is important to consider the goals of such training. What do we want to accomplish with a readers' advisory training program? Training of readers' advisors should accomplish the goals listed in Figure 7.1. Because these goals form the basis of training activities, it is important to consider them individually in more detail.

The Goals of Readers' Advisory Training

Teaching staff to understand and acknowledge the importance of readers' advisory service in the public library constitutes the first training goal. Not all of us are fortunate enough to have staff and administration committed to the idea that the fiction collection is as important as any other part of the library collection. Staff and administration must understand that when we do not provide assistance to the fiction collection, we essentially deny service to a large part of our clientele, readers who are responsible for more than a third of the average public library's book circulation. Readers' advisory questions are fundamentally no different from any other reference question. We need to acknowledge this fact and help staff to understand it as well. As library professionals, we pride ourselves on the level of service we provide to our nonfiction collections, but fiction too often remains a self-service collection. In most libraries, no other single adult collection accounts for such a high percentage of total circulation. Therefore, we should actively train staff to help patrons with their inquiries, and we should support the collection with reference sources and guides that allow both staff and readers to use it more effectively. Staff must learn to acknowledge that the patron asking for a book that is "just like" those Stephen King writes deserves the same level of service as the person who wants information on building a deck.

This is not always an easy concept to accept. Over the years, we have all encountered many justifications for this denial of service to fiction readers. We may argue we are too busy with "legitimate" reference questions to handle readers' advisory requests, which, because they involve the fiction collection, are somehow "illegitimate" and not worthy of consideration. Or we may complain that there are too often no straightforward, easy-to-find answers to readers' advisory queries. A reference book will not give a long list of books just like those by Stephen King. To help the reader who asks for more books "just like" King writes, we need to discover what it is about King that the reader enjoys before we can identify similar titles, and even then reference sources are often deficient. It takes time to become familiar enough with fiction genres to be able to help readers. That there is often no training and that there are few reference sources make these questions seem even more difficult. A third argument can be summarized in the frequently heard justification, "We don't get questions like that at our reference desk, so why bother learning about the fiction collection." Since libraries in general have worked hard to teach patrons over the years that asking for a good book is an inappropriate question, we should not wonder at the lack of queries.

The biggest deterrent, in our experience, is that many of us really are too busy to answer all questions in the detail they deserve.

That readers' advisory questions are not straightforward makes them seem even more difficult and time-consuming. However, no other collection is actively excluded from reference instruction and training in the way that fiction is. We do not single out any other questions or groups of users and say we will not handle their queries. Libraries are deluged with difficult health and business questions, but we have never heard of a library that has designated those as areas in which questions simply will not be answered. Until we are also willing to say we will not answer business or health or any other group of questions because we are too busy or the questions are too complicated, we need to reconsider the appropriateness of doing just that to fiction questions. Thus, the first goal of readers' advisory training is to provide tools—physical and intellectual—that allow us to answer fiction questions just as we handle all other reference questions. Staff must learn to see readers' advisory as an *integral part of their job responsibilities* in order to provide good reference service as well as good public service.

Once we accept the inherent necessity of providing readers' advisory service, we need to ensure that staff are comfortable, skilled, and nonjudgmental in their interactions. This is the second training goal. Betty Rosenberg's motto, *Never apologize for your reading tastes,* should set the tone for all readers' advisory activities and interactions. We all know that if readers ask for titles and authors we dislike or find frivolous, and if we let our attitude show, those readers will never ask again. Nor will any patron who overhears the interaction. We do not have to *like* everything, but we must find phrases to use in talking about materials we do not enjoy so that we can preserve our own integrity, yet acknowledge what it is about a type of fiction, an author, or a title that a reader finds enjoyable.

The third training goal is that readers' advisors must learn to discover what an individual reader is looking for—to move from readers to books—not from books we have personally enjoyed to every reader who asks for suggestions. Readers' advisory work would be so much easier if there were an infinite list of perfect books that would satisfy every reader who asks for suggestions, or even if we could simply keep a stack of the last book we really enjoyed and pass it out to everyone who asks for suggestions. Our job might be easier, but readers are unlikely to leave satisfied. Readers expect us to suggest titles that meet their own personal reading needs and interests. We need to learn to do this and to teach our staff how to do it as well.

Finally, we strongly believe, after years of working directly with fiction readers, that readers read for more than just plot or subject. They also look for books with similar appeal elements, which were discussed in detail in chapter 3. Staff must learn to describe books by appeal, not just by plot, because, as we have discovered, appeal-based descriptions allow readers to more readily make choices about what they are in the mood to read. Describing books by appeal also relieves us of the task of remembering the plot line of every book we talk about. Relying on appeal not only capitalizes on strategies we naturally employ in sharing books but also makes recalling and describing books easier. If we have mastered the techniques described in chapters 3 and 4 and learned to be alert to appeal elements in all we read and hear about books, we greatly expand the range of books we can discuss with patrons.

Training and supervising staff place an enormous responsibility on those of us in charge of these activities. We feel strongly that trainers and supervisors should also work the desk and model appropriate behaviors and techniques. We must teach and reinforce public service skills in order to show, as well as to tell, staff how to be nonjudgmental, positive, enthusiastic, and professional in all our interactions. We also must help staff fit readers' advisory into their desk responsibilities and help them become comfortable sharing books so this activity becomes automatic, a part of their daily routine.

Basic Training
for Readers' Advisors

In training new staff, it is important to recognize and acknowledge what seem to be two of their greatest fears:

> How can I ever read enough so that I can talk
> with readers?
>
> How can I remember what I do read?

It is all too easy for new staff to become overwhelmed. They shadow us in the stacks and hear us talking—knowledgeably, they assume—with a range of readers, whose tastes run the gamut from Cyberpunk to Henry James. No wonder they are concerned! It is important to reassure new staff, to make clear to them from the first that there are strategies to use in working with fiction readers, that they will be taught these techniques, that providing readers' advisory is not as impossible as it may seem, and that we all felt overwhelmed

Figure 7.2
Basic Skills for Readers' Advisors

1. How to build on and expand their knowledge of fiction.
2. How to think about books.
3. How to talk about books.
4. How to use reference sources.
5. How to write about books

at first. Then we need to embark on training activities that help staff become comfortable and allay their fears.

We have found that beginning readers' advisors need to master five basic skills, listed in Figure 7.2, during the first year of training. Figure 7.3 illustrates A Checklist for Readers' Advisory Training, which describes these skills and provides activities that can be used to teach them. This model can be readily adapted to meet an individual library's training and staff needs. Such a tool is useful for both trainer and new staff since it lays out the activities, in approximate order, that will constitute the training process. This example of a training program is specifically correlated to this book and thus requires reading, discussion, and exercises described in the previous chapters. This is a model to be adapted to meet a library's specific training needs. If your library lacks a training checklist, we advise you to take this as an example and adapt it to meet your own needs. At the Downers Grove Public Library, readers' advisory training takes place after all other desk and reference training. One staff member oversees this training, acting as a mentor. In addition to regularly scheduled formal meetings, he or she touches base with the new staff member informally for five to ten minutes every week. Although one person is responsible for the training, all in the department benefit from this skills refresher course as everyone, at some point, works with the new staff member, either on desk or informally in the workroom, responding to questions and sharing favorite reference sources and authors. New staff learn early on that the best readers' advisory is not done in a vacuum; it is a team effort and involves sharing resources and techniques, not to mention books.

Figure 7.3
A Checklist for Readers' Advisory Training

Assignment	Date	Discussed/Initials
Assess reading background	_____	_____
Design reading plan and set discussion dates	_____	_____
Keep track of what is read	_____	_____
Appeal:		
Read and discuss chapter 3	_____	_____
Description exercise	_____	_____
Book summaries	_____	_____
Readers' advisory interview:		
Read and discuss chapter 4	_____	_____
Read Hanff and Morley	_____	_____
Reference sources and questions:		
Read and discuss chapter 2	_____	_____
Peruse collection of department book lists and bookmarks	_____	_____
Departmental annotation form:		
Read and discuss chapter 5	_____	_____
Unannotated bookmark:		
Read and discuss chapter 6	_____	_____
Annotated book list	_____	_____
Philosophy of service:		
Read and discuss chapter 1	_____	_____

Assignment	Date	Discussed/Initials
On-desk activities:		
Keeping track of questions	_____	_____
Setting interview goals	_____	_____
Filling Good Books truck	_____	_____
Filling displays	_____	_____

The first step in the training process is to teach new staff how to build on and expand their knowledge of fiction, especially popular fiction. We start here to address and help counteract that fear of not having read enough. Our Popular Fiction List (see Appendix) serves as the basis for an assessment of the new staff member's knowledge of popular fiction and the formulation of a reading plan. This list reflects the thirteen most popular genres at our library and, within each genre, the twelve most popular authors. Having new staff initial names of the authors they have read serves two purposes: First, they can easily see how much they really have read and know something about, and second, we trainers can see where to start in setting up a reading plan to expand that knowledge. We discussed Designing a Reading Plan in more detail in chapter 5. There are many ways to do this, depending on our schedules, our expectations, and the other reading assignments in which the new employees will be expected to join. For example, we might assign a book a month and then discuss it; or we might assign two or three books with a longer reading time, again followed by a scheduled discussion. We start new readers' advisors in a genre popular with patrons so they will be able to use their knowledge immediately as they interact with readers. At first, the trainer should assume responsibility for selecting the titles to be read in order to guarantee they are typical of the author's writing. Later, when staff are comfortable using reference and staff resources to choose typical titles, they take on that responsibility themselves.

The scheduled discussion is the second part of this exercise. It is not enough simply to read popular authors and titles; readers' advisors need to learn first what to look for as they read, then how to think about books and, finally, how to talk about books with readers. Thus, the reading plan with its concomitant discussion prepares the way for later training activities. When we meet to talk about books, we do not structure our conversation like a formal book discussion, and we do not talk about what is good or bad about a book or author. Instead, we focus on questions such as those listed in Figure 5.5, which emphasize what an author does best; thus, we help staff see the appeal even of books they personally do not enjoy. These might seem like a lot of questions for new staff to try to consider, but these questions reflect the thinking that makes us better readers' advisors and helps new staff understand what to look for and focus on as they read. A list of possible questions to consider helps new staff focus more easily on what they need to be aware of and makes their reading assignment more manageable, not to mention comprehensible. Needless to say, staff become more skilled at responding to this directed reading as they progress through their training, but these questions provide an initial framework and direction. They help new staff see how to think and then talk about books they are reading, and the questions help staff focus their energy.

At this point, we also encourage staff to keep track of what they read, simply by recording authors and titles in a notebook. This is discussed in detail in chapter 4. Later, we encourage more formal and detailed methods of keeping notes on books, described in chapter 5, but simply listing titles and authors in order is the initial step. Staff will soon realize the almost magical properties of this technique in their increased ability to remember what they have read. It is tempting to forgo such a simple step, but comments by readers and readers' advisors over the past ten years have reinforced the importance of this activity as a valuable tool. Keeping a list and reviewing it sustain and reinforce the pleasure many of us find in reading and underscore the importance of offering a service that recognizes and promotes such pleasure.

As we mentioned earlier, the two greatest fears new staff face are not being able to read enough and not remembering what they have read. Setting up a reading plan, with time to discuss the titles read, addresses the first issue and sets the stage for confronting the second. Remembering what we have read does seem to become easier when it is our *job* to remember, but keeping track of what we read helps us remember more, as well. The key to remembering more of what we read, however, is to think in terms of the appeal of a book, rather than its plot. As trainers, we need to demonstrate that books are more than plots or subjects and that patrons are usually seeking a book with a particular feel rather than one on a specific subject.

We presented the idea of appeal in depth in chapter 3 and discussed its role in preparing for the readers' advisory interview in chapter 4. Almost ten years after this book was originally written, we feel even more strongly that appeal plays the most important role both in reading enjoyment and preference in future selections. We have seen that thinking about a book in terms of its appeal, rather than a plot summary, helps us remember more. Sharing a book in terms of appeal not only reflects the way we naturally talk about books but also allows readers to make choices more readily. Staff need to learn to read for appeal and to use appeal to share books more effectively. Figures 3.1 through 3.4 list questions to think about when considering a book's appeal. Practice makes these thought processes more automatic, and readers' satisfaction with these appeal-based suggestions reinforces their importance.

Mastering appeal also allows us to look at books we have not read and glean the same kinds of useful information we gain from reading. At this point in their training, staff also learn how to scan book jackets and reviews to find clues to appeal, as well as how to abstract similar information from readers' comments about books they have read. None of us will ever be able to read enough to meet the diverse and changing interests of all the readers we help. Staff must learn to gather information from a range of print and reader comments and use that information to expand their own knowledge.

An understanding of appeal forms the basis for the way readers' advisors think about books. It also provides a format to use in talking about books. There is an art to the way readers' advisors need to talk about books, and we are more successful when we learn to formulate our comments in terms of appeal rather than plot summaries. Learning to talk about books requires practice, first with staff and then with patrons. New staff are meeting formally with their trainer to discuss reading assignments on a scheduled basis. Talking about books informally should be an integral aspect of the department's routine, a natural activity, a part of the regular interaction in the workroom and at the desk. All talking about books helps; it makes us conscious of appeal, of what makes the book popular beyond its subject or genre. Talking informally among staff allows us to practice structuring our comments in terms of appeal, to discover and share phrases that are effective, to become more comfortable sharing books so that we will be at ease working with patrons. Talking among the staff also reinforces that this is a legitimate activity for readers' advisors to engage in, and it emphasizes the importance of sharing information. Successful readers' advisory requires a team effort. The more a department works as a team, sharing books and techniques, asking each other for help and information, the better readers' advisory service we provide, and the better public service staff we become. The Morley and Hanff books discussed in chapter 4 emphasize the pleasure gained from sharing books.

Talking about books with patrons was discussed in depth in chapter 4. From a training perspective, we need to underscore the idea that the readers' advisory interview is a *conversation* about books between staff and patrons, with questions and suggestions handed back and forth. We suggest books based on what patrons say they enjoy reading, and we encourage them to come back for more, to let us know whether they enjoyed the books or not. As talking about books with staff becomes part of their routine, new staff become more comfortable talking with patrons as well. We train them to conduct successful readers' advisory interviews, covered in depth in chapter 4. Many of the Special Situations, also discussed in chapter 4, relate to this training stage. Talking over these problems and suggested techniques for solving them increases the comfort level for new staff. They learn that all of us experience these situations, and they gain skill and confidence in dealing with them. They begin to develop their own sensible strategies to deal with potentially difficult situations. We help them develop and practice nonjudgmental phrases to use in talking about authors or genres they do not personally enjoy. Role-playing may be a useful exercise at this stage to help new staff feel more comfortable and prepare for interactions with patrons.

We offer three tips to help make the readers' advisory interview more manageable. First, there is no perfect book. Our job in working with readers is not to find the one and only perfect book that will suit them that day; we suggest a range of titles that might appeal to this reader. Second, we reinforce the distinction between suggesting and recommending. In a library situation, we suggest several books that might appeal, based on what the patron has said about reading taste and mood. Finally, we emphasize that the point of the interview is to get the patron to talk, and we try to give new staff lines to use as suggestions of ways to elicit information. We remind staff not to ask, What do you like to read? A request such as, Tell me about a book you have enjoyed, encourages readers to talk. We reinforce that readers' advisory reference is not just books; it may be other staff, consulting on questions and calling readers back with answers or suggestions, as well as the annotated book lists or bookmarks staff have created.

We also begin setting goals for readers' advisory interactions every time new staff are scheduled at the desk. When they consistently meet their goals, it is time to increase them by one or two. Just as we keep tally of reference questions for library statistics, we should keep track of readers' advisory interactions. Keeping statistics is important, if only for the personal satisfaction of seeing the growing number of readers who seek assistance. Statistics can also provide a tangible record of goals set and met. For example, we encourage a new readers' advisor to set a goal of two readers' advisory interactions during each four-hour on-desk shift. When that goal is comfortably met, it should be increased. Setting goals reminds us to approach and talk with patrons about books, even when we are busy at the desk. Then, just as we encourage staff to keep track of what they read, we have them keep a log of their readers' advisory interviews. They discuss these—problems and successes—with their trainer.

Introduction to readers' advisory reference sources constitutes the next training step. These resources were discussed in detail in chapter 2. It is useful to have a list of the library's readers' advisory reference sources so staff can methodically review each source, examining indexes, coverage, tone of articles, and ease of use. We assign sample questions at this point. Figure 7.4 lists examples of assigned questions. Questions should be designed to highlight the range of material contained in the most useful sources, as well as to direct staff to the more obscure tools. In most cases, there is not one correct source but rather several resources in which the answer can be found. In talking over the questions and answers, we trainers can make suggestions about the best sources and share strategies we find useful. While it is important for new staff to work primarily with a specific trainer, at this point they benefit greatly from discussing reference questions and sources with all staff who work the desk. Just as we share information about books we read, we share tips for handling readers' advisory reference questions and hints about special features found in these sources. We all have favorite sources, just as we have favorite authors; new staff benefit from all our suggestions and experiences. Remember, among the library's best resources may be book lists and bookmarks developed by staff in response to reader interests and requests. New staff should be

Figure 7.4
Readers' Advisory Assignment

---

1. Who is the series character that owns a bookstore in the Joan Hess mysteries?

2. I would like to read some books set in Chicago—nothing too heavy. Can you suggest any?

3. I need a short book to read for a high school book report due tomorrow. Can you find me a list?

4. I think I have read all the Robert Ludlum books. I heard he wrote under another name. Can you find out what it was and the books written under that name?

5. I want to read the Jalna series in order. Can you tell me what are the first two books in the series?

6. I would like to read some fiction books set in Australia in the 1700s.

7. Who wrote the science fiction robot series? You know, the ones where the author lists the rules for robots.

8. There is a series of mysteries in which the detective is a dwarf. Who wrote them, and what is the detective's name?

9. I like thrillers, you know—spies, intrigue. Can you suggest any funny titles?

10. I heard that Louis L'Amour wrote Hopalong Cassidy novels. Is that true? What are the titles? Did he use his own name?

11. I want to start reading Edith Wharton. Which novel would you suggest I start with?

12. I like Robert Silverberg's books, but I think I have read everything he has written. Who else writes like him?

---

familiar with these as well, since they are a resource that patrons can take with them and refer to later.

At the Downers Grove Public Library, we start working with reference sources and questions when new staff begin to sit the desk with us and shadow us on reference and readers' advisory questions. Once staff are assigned to the desk alone, they continue to keep track of questions asked and sources consulted so these can be discussed at weekly meetings with their trainer.

Writing about books is the last of the basic training skills. When hired, staff are informed they will be required to read and annotate two books monthly. The format for annotations, along with the book sheet that staff records notes on while reading, were covered in Figures 5.2 and 5.4. Writing gives precision to our comments about a book and its appeal. It helps clear up any muddiness we experience when talking about books, and it forces us to think specifically in terms of appeal and similar authors readers might enjoy. In addition to writing the monthly annotations, within their first year new staff prepare an unannotated bookmark and begin work on an annotated book list. Details of both these projects were discussed in chapter 6, Promotion.

Although understanding and acknowledging the importance of providing readers' advisory is essential, a discussion of the philosophy of providing the service is usually left for later in the training, when new staff have a sense of the kind of work involved and can better relate to the ideas that structure the service.

After all this, there is another topic we feel it is vital that we address: How do we keep new staff from feeling overwhelmed? When they see all there is to learn and recognize all they do not know, the first reaction of many beginning readers' advisors is panic and fear that they can never do this job. We all have days when we feel there is no hope, that we can never read enough, never remember what we have read, never figure out why an author appeals to readers, and never be able to talk comfortably with patrons. It helps to recognize that we cannot read everything—that reading everything is not even our goal. What we are doing is reading and learning about key authors and titles so we develop a frame of reference that allows us to interact successfully with readers. One way to counteract this feeling of inadequacy is to encourage staff to regularly take stock of what they have done. Check off authors on the Popular Fiction List; look back over their reading record; realize that they can increase their goal for readers' advisory interviews; work on annotations, bookmarks, and book lists; and/or review all they have learned from studying a genre. All this helps readers' advisors—beginning and experienced—to see how far they have come.

Initial training of readers' advisors involves providing mental and physical tools. The former includes ways to think and talk about books; the latter covers reference sources, annotations, and bibliographies. We also provide reassurance and strategies for dealing with difficult problems, and we set up situations in which success is likely by providing a reading plan and opportunities to make talking about books part of their routine, even before new staff work with readers.

Ongoing Training for Readers' Advisors

While basic readers' advisory training provides tools and techniques to help staff become familiar with resources and comfortable working with patrons, ongoing training is designed to stimulate and motivate experienced staff, to keep them fresh and intellectually challenged in their work. Useful activities, summarized in Figure 7.5, help meet this goal.

Just as a reading plan provides the basis for initial training, so it can stimulate more experienced readers' advisors. We use the same basic techniques discussed in chapter 5, selecting a popular genre with which the staff member is less familiar or may not enjoy, then reading and discussing specific titles to discover more about an author or genre's appeal. This is an activity that can be done with two or more staff, making it a mini–genre study, or with a staff

Figure 7.5
Ongoing Training Activities for Experienced Readers' Advisors

1. Design a personal reading plan.
2. Read in unfamiliar genres.
3. Read authors on the best-sellers lists.
4. Share discoveries with staff and patrons.
5. Practice talking about books—every day.
6. Collect and share "sure bets."
7. Keep statistics of readers' advisory interviews and set personal goals to increase interactions.
8. Create annotated book lists.
9. Brainstorm similar author bookmarks for popular authors.
10. Create readers' advisory tools such as a Popular Fiction List.
11. Undertake a genre study.

member and another reader. It is even possible to do this on one's own, but we feel we need the stimulation of the discussion of a book's appeal to gain the greatest benefit. In any case, talking about what we are reading or what we have learned about specific authors and titles from other sources must be part of the daily routine of all in an active and successful readers' advisory department.

Staff should also be encouraged to read authors on the best-sellers list. We used to require staff to read all titles on the best-sellers list. Now we simply require familiarity with the authors and/or titles. Since most authors on these lists have appeared previously, it is necessary to read only new authors or books by best-selling authors if they pursue new directions. Still, staff need to be aware of and familiar with best-selling authors, because many patrons come to the library looking for their books. We need to know something about them and, more important, other authors to suggest when the best-sellers are checked out and unavailable. If they make a point of discovering these similar authors, knowledgeable staff, interested in helping readers find other titles to tide them over until their turn for a best-seller, can set up readers' advisory relationships that encourage readers to return for more suggestions later.

Experienced readers' advisors should also set personal goals to increase their number of readers' advisory interactions when they are on the desk. While more readers approach the desk and request book suggestions in libraries with established readers' advisory services, we still need to encourage staff to check with readers in the book stacks and offer assistance. Setting goals reminds us to offer book suggestions, to talk with patrons in the stacks to ensure that all library users are finding the information they seek in both fiction and nonfiction collections.

Creating annotated book lists affords an opportunity for staff to explore a topic in depth and produce a resource valuable to fellow staff members and patrons. We encourage staff to work on one every year, following the process outlined in chapter 6. Occasionally, we work as a team to produce book lists on topics or in genres no single staff member is interested in or willing to tackle on her own or to compile results of a genre study. Staff still benefit from the discussions to select titles, from their own reading and annotation writing, and from the finished book list, which becomes a readers' advisory reference source. Staff can also cooperate to brainstorm similar-author bookmarks for some of our most popular authors, who will never be able to write enough to satisfy their many fans. This process was discussed in detail in chapter 6.

Devising our own readers' advisory resources also offers useful training opportunities. If your library does not have a Popular Fiction List, you should consider taking ours (see Appendix) apart and creating your own. This activity, described in chapter 2, provides an excellent training exercise for staff, as does updating and revising an already existing list. In constructing a Popular Fiction List, we must consider which authors truly are the most popular in our library and be able to justify our decision. In fact, updating our list has become an annual departmental training activity. In preparation, we review the current version of the list, considering which authors are still popular and which have become less so. We make a special effort to research authors who have become more popular in the past year and may now belong on the list. Reviewing best-sellers lists, tracking authors included in our Rental Books collection (always among the most popular), and checking reserve queues prepare us for the discussion—sometimes almost a battle—to see which authors are to remain on the list. Afterward, we have an up-to-date list that truly reflects the most popular authors our patrons read, and the process itself hones our skills in gathering information about what our patrons are reading.

Designing library-specific readers' advisory reference sources is a particularly valuable training exercise. Experienced readers' advisors can also find areas in which reference sources fall short and for which a specialized tool—a data base or even a book list—can make the collection more accessible. For example, when we needed a reliable, up-to-date resource that identified fantasy books in series, a staff member set up a data base with this information, and our high school aides now update it. The listing—by title, series title, and author—is printed out regularly, and readers, especially a growing group of high school fans, consult it frequently.

Participation in a genre study constitutes the last, as well as the most advanced and time-consuming, of the ongoing training activities. As discussed in chapter 5, genre studies provide a way to learn about popular authors and the genres in which they write. To begin, we choose a high-demand genre, one both patrons and staff enjoy. We read in the genre and about the genre; then we discuss our discoveries at regularly scheduled meetings. We formulate a list of genre characteristics early on and refine it as we read. During the process, we identify benchmark authors and discover what it is that characterizes their work. Then we compare other authors to these benchmarks and create appeal-based subgenres with unique characteristics and a list of authors who seem to fit together within them.

All of this takes time—to read, react, discuss—and considerable effort. It requires commitment and dedication. Could the benefits possibly justify the work involved? One important reason to study genres is that many, if not most, of our library patrons are genre readers, and this in-depth study has immediate benefits both in our expanded knowledge of a particular genre and in our increased ability to recognize patterns and similar authors in all fiction we read. By identifying the appeal of the genre and discovering key authors within subgenres, we can also identify similar authors and become a valuable resource to readers.

Although a genre study requires an enormous amount of reading, reacting, and discussion, it also provides a large measure of intellectual satisfaction and enjoyment. Its participatory nature involves sharing books and fosters the pleasure inherent in this activity. Studying a genre requires us to read and think about authors in terms of their appeal. No matter what genre we are studying, these benefits carry over into all our other reading and conversations with patrons. Information in reference books about an author or genre does not provide answers to questions about the nature of their appeal. We discover those answers when we take what we have read and combine it with what we have gained from our conversation with staff and other readers. We begin making important and useful connections; it is a very satisfying experience.

When we are focusing on a genre, we begin to have more interesting and satisfying conversations with readers as well. Our readers' advisory interview skills grow because we are asking readers questions that reflect what we want to discover about a genre. We become more aware of readers, books, and appeal elements. As we read a particular genre, we provide better readers' advisory suggestions for the fans of that genre, but we also do better readers' advisory in general because we are more aware of readers and the appeal elements they enjoy.

Genre study generates a certain excitement among the participants. In addition to the heightened awareness when we read and talk with patrons, there is the excitement of the chase, of following clues, and then of pulling all the information together. We find ourselves writing down bits from reviews or reference books—lines that characterize an author—and then tracking them down to see if they are correct and what they mean in terms of the pattern we have described for the genre.

Genre studies are also great confidence builders. As we read and explore a genre, we gain assurance from our growing knowledge and become more comfortable sharing what we have learned with patrons and soliciting their opinions. These conversations pique our curiosity so that we read further and discuss more comfortably. Genre studies are a jumping-off point for more experienced readers' advisors, a springboard from which more extensive work with readers and books is launched.

In addition, having studied one genre, we have a framework to use as we approach other, unfamiliar genres. Even though every genre study unfolds differently, we gain a sense of where to start and how to progress and comfortably apply our general knowledge of the process to this new situation with satisfying results.

Finally, genre study is an activity to be enjoyed. The pleasure in unraveling puzzles is one of the elements of reference and readers' advisory that has attracted many of us, and genre study is one of the best ways to experience this. Reading a genre to discover its pattern, reading books within genres to understand why they appeal to readers, and seeking other books and authors with the same appeal are stimulating exercises that provide both intellectual challenge and enjoyment.

Devoting a chapter of this book to training goals and techniques emphasizes the necessity of a firm commitment from both library administration and staff to providing this service. Obviously, in order to provide even the most rudimentary service, readers' advisors must make a commitment of time and effort. We need preparation time to master the techniques of the readers' advisory interview, to learn to talk about books with readers, to gain familiarity with the broad range of popular fiction, and to create tools to help readers' advisors assist patrons. A willingness to read—and to read widely—must be a prerequisite for all readers' advisory staff. However, even a staff composed of readers must make an additional commitment to expand the scope of their reading in order to gain the best background.

Administratively, it is important to acknowledge this commitment to a service that requires extensive preparation by providing library time, whenever possible, for reading and for creating tools to use with patrons and staff. Scheduled work time away from the service desk is a necessity. Readers' advisors need time to concentrate on developing the complex skills that are necessary to provide a comprehensive readers' advisory service.

In a library committed to providing readers' advisory, staff also need time and opportunity to offer the service to patrons. If the reference or circulation staff—or any public service staff that also provides other library services—provides readers' advisory, there is always the danger that readers' advisory, because it often lacks the immediacy of reference, circulation, or other transactions, will receive short shrift. Care must be taken to avoid this possibility and to acknowledge and promote the readers' advisory service. In a library that *does* commit itself to readers' advisory service, readers begin to see librarians as a reading resource, and readers' advisors become a very satisfying link in the chain connecting books and readers.

Since this chapter addresses the training of staff who work with fiction, we want to conclude by quoting not from a management text, but from a work of fiction. In *No Witnesses,* by Ridley Pearson, his series detective, Lou Boldt, is teaching a police course in investigative techniques. At the end of the class, Boldt realizes,

> There comes a time when all the information must be set aside; there comes a time when passion and instinct take over. It's the stuff that can't be taught; but it can be learned.[1]

That encapsulates what we feel about training readers' advisors. We can provide reference tools and training exercises and more, but we cannot force staff to learn how to make connections between readers and books. With the right inspiration and a good grounding in basic techniques, however, the art of readers' advisory can be learned. We, as supervisors and trainers, are facilitators in this process; whatever we do and however we do it, we are forging links in the chains of readers who skillfully share their pleasure in reading.

Note

1. Ridley Pearson, *No Witnesses* (New York: Hyperion, 1994), 1–2.

▚▚▚▚ BIBLIOGRAPHY

Selected Historical Sources

Carrier, Esther Jane. *Fiction in Public Libraries, 1876–1900.* Lanham, Md.: Scarecrow, 1965.

————. *Fiction in Public Libraries, 1900–1950.* Littleton, Colo: Libraries Unlimited, 1985.

Chancellor, John, Miriam D. Tompkins, and Hazel I. Medway. *Helping the Reader toward Self-education.* Chicago: American Library Assn., 1938.

Doud, Margery. *The Readers' Advisory Service of the St. Louis Public Library.* St. Louis, Mo.: St. Louis Public Library, 1929.

Flexner, Jennie M., and Sigrid A. Edge. *A Readers' Advisory Service.* New York: American Assn. for Adult Education, 1934.

Flexner, Jennie M., and Byron C. Hopkins. *Readers' Advisers at Work: A Survey of Development in the New York Public Library.* New York: American Assn. for Adult Education, 1941.

Foster, Jeannette Howard. "An Approach to Fiction through the Characteristics of Its Readers." *Library Quarterly* 6 (April 1936): 124–74.

Lee, Robert Ellis. *Continuing Education for Adults through the American Public Library, 1833–1964.* Chicago: American Library Assn., 1966.

Lyman, Helen Huguenor. *Readers' Guidance Service in a Small Public Library.* Chicago: American Library Assn., 1962.

Regan, Lee. "Status of Readers' Advisory Service." *RQ* 12 (Spring 1973): 227–33.

Shortt, May. "Advisers Anonymous, Arise!" *Ontario Library Review* 59 (May 1965): 81–83.

Popular Fiction List

Crime/Caper

Caunitz, William J.
Connelly, Michael
Hall, James W.
Hiaasen, Carl
Leonard, Elmore
Lindsey, David
Perry, Thomas
Sanders, Lawrence
Shames, Laurence
Wambaugh, Joseph
Westlake, Donald E.
Woods, Stuart

Fantasy

Anthony, Piers
Asprin, Robert Lynn
Bradley, Marion Zimmer
Brooks, Terry
Eddings, David

Feist, Raymond E.
Goodkind, Terry
Jordan, Robert
Kurtz, Katherine
Lackey, Mercedes
Rawn, Melanie
Weis, Margaret

Gentle Reads

Beaton, M. C. (M)
Binchy, Maeve
Ibbotson, Eva
Karon, Jan
MacLeod, Charlotte (M)
Morris, Gilbert
Oke, Janette
Pilcher, Rosamunde
Purser, Ann
Read, Miss
Whitnell, Barbara
Williams, Jeanne

Literature and Audio Services Department
Downers Grove Public Library, 1997
May Not Be Reproduced without Permission

Historical and Historical Storyteller

Auel, Jean M.
Belle, Pamela
Cornwell, Bernard
Gabaldon, Diana
George, Margaret
Laker, Rosalind
Michener, James A.
O'Brian, Patrick
Penman, Sharon Kay
Plain, Belva
Price, Eugenia
Roberson, Jennifer

Horror

Barker, Clive
Farris, John
Gaiman, Neil
King, Stephen
Koontz, Dean R.
McCammon, Robert R.
Newman, Kim
Rice, Anne
Saul, John
Simmons, Dan
Straub, Peter
Strieber, Whitley

Literary Fiction

Brown, Rosellen
Conroy, Pat
Gibbons, Kaye
Godwin, Gail
Hoffman, Alice
McMurtry, Larry
Miller, Sue
Morrison, Toni
Oates, Joyce Carol

Smiley, Jane
Tan, Amy
Tyler, Anne

Mystery/Detective

Block, Lawrence
Braun, Lilian Jackson
Burke, James Lee
Cornwell, Patricia D.
Davidson, Diane Mott
George, Elizabeth
Grafton, Sue
Hillerman, Tony
McBain, Ed
Parker, Robert B.
Perry, Anne
Peters, Elizabeth

Romance and Romantic Storyteller

Adler, Elizabeth
Brown, Sandra
Chesney, Marion
Coulter, Catherine
Deveraux, Jude
Garwood, Julie
Jayne Ann Krentz/
  Amanda Quick
Lowell, Elizabeth
McNaught, Judith
Roberts, Nora
Spencer, LaVyrle
Stone, Katherine

Science Fiction

Adams, Douglas
Anthony, Piers
Asimov, Isaac
Bradbury, Ray

Card, Orson Scott
Clarke, Arthur C.
Harrison, Harry
McCaffrey, Anne
Niven, Larry
Shatner, William
Star Trek and Star Trek
    The Next Generation
Star Wars

Storyteller

Archer, Jeffrey
Browne, Gerald A.
Crichton, Michael
De Mille, Nelson
Diehl, William
Follett, Ken
Griffin, W.E.B.
Grisham, John
Krantz, Judith
Martini, Stephen
Sheldon, Sidney
Turow, Scott

Suspense and Romantic Suspense

Allegretto, Michael
Clark, Mary Higgins
Cook, Robin
Fielding, Joy
Kellerman, Jonathan
Klavan, Andrew
Margolin, Phillip
Michaels, Barbara

Patterson, James
Robards, Karen
Sandford, John
Wiltse, David

Adventure/Espionage

Brown, Dale
Clancy, Tom
Coonts, Stephen
Cussler, Clive
Deighton, Len
Forsyth, Frederick
Gardner, John
Higgins, Jack
Iles, Greg
le Carré, John
Ludlum, Robert
Seymour, Gerald

Women's Lives and Relationships

Berg, Elizabeth
Bradford, Barbara Taylor
Chamberlain, Diane
Delinsky, Barbara
Goldsmith, Olivia
Isaacs, Susan
Kingsolver, Barbara
Michaels, Fern
Mortman, Doris
Rice, Luanne
Siddons, Anne Rivers
Steel, Danielle
Thayer, Nancy

FICTION AUTHOR INDEX

SUBJECT INDEX

Joyce G. Saricks has been the literature and audio services coordinator at the Downers Grove (Illinois) Public Library since 1983, when she and Nancy Brown created a readers' advisory service there. With Nancy Brown and alone, Joyce Saricks has presented more than forty workshops on readers' advisory for public libraries and library systems. In addition, she has spoken at eleven state and regional library conferences, as well as seven national library conferences. Joyce Saricks was the 1989 recipient of the Public Library Association's Allie Beth Martin Award, which honors "an extraordinary range and depth of knowledge about books or other library materials and . . . a distinguished ability to share that knowledge." In 1995, she was named Librarian of the Year for Northern Illinois by the Windy City Romance Writers.